M

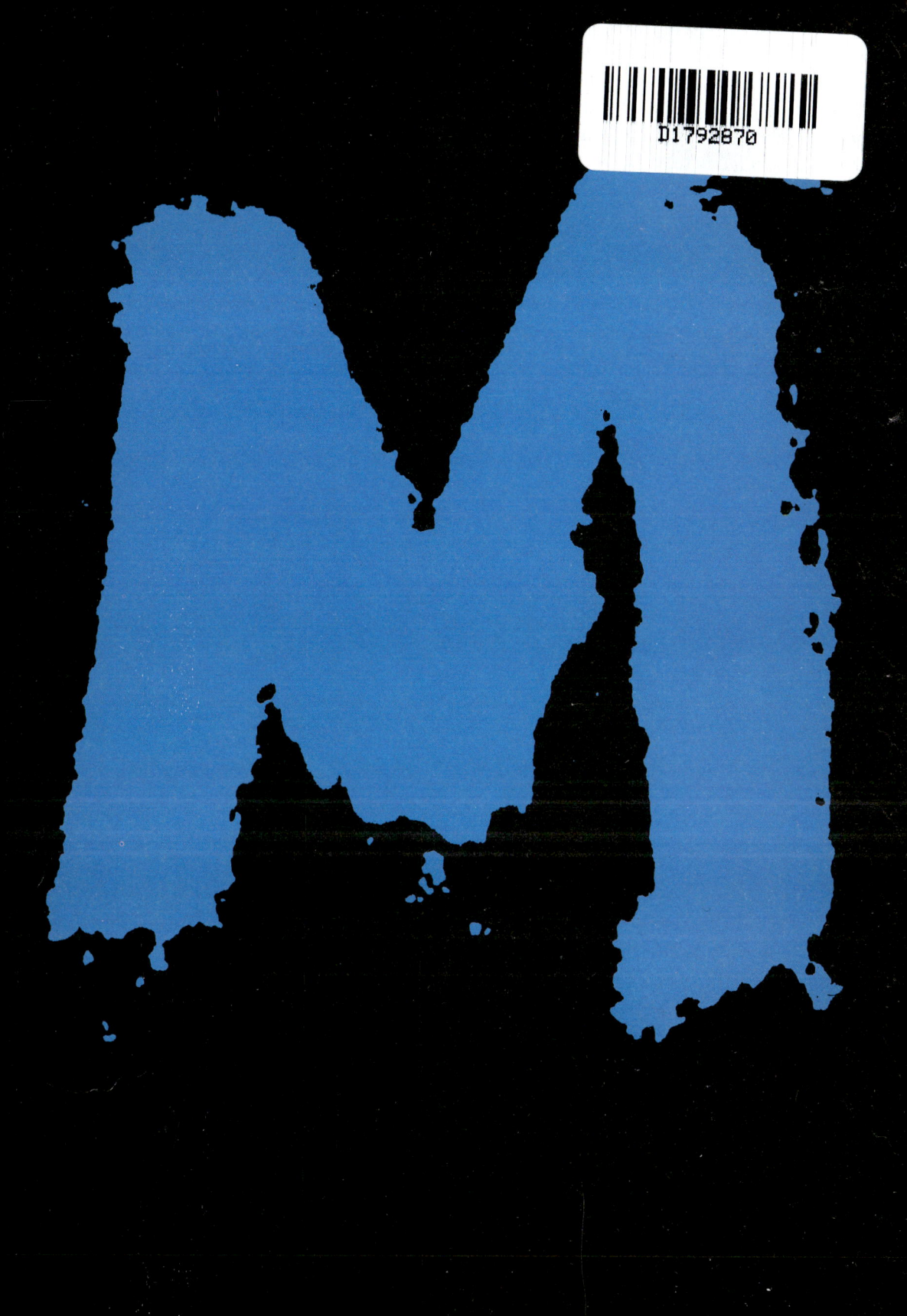

When the frustrated, stymied police begin to raid all the criminal hideouts, rounding up thieves, prostitutes, and beggars, the criminals, masterminded by Schranker, decide to take the matter into their own hands and find the murderer themselves. The criminals make use of the Beggars' Guild (a union of street beggars) to comb the city. Meanwhile, with evidence produced through the investigations of Lohmann and Inspector Groeber, the police have staked out the apartment of the man they believe to be the killer. A blind balloon seller, by chance, identifies the murderer by the Grieg tune he is fond of whistling and alerts his colleagues by having a friend imprint the letter M in chalk on the culprit's back. The murderer is pursued and the beggars corner him in the railroad yards; just as he is about to be apprehended. . .he mysteriously vanishes.

M

a book by Jon J Muth

edited by Steve Niles

based on the film by Fritz Lang

with script by Thea Von Harbou

THE HUNTING
B O O K   T H R E E

For Julianna

ECLIPSE BOOKS

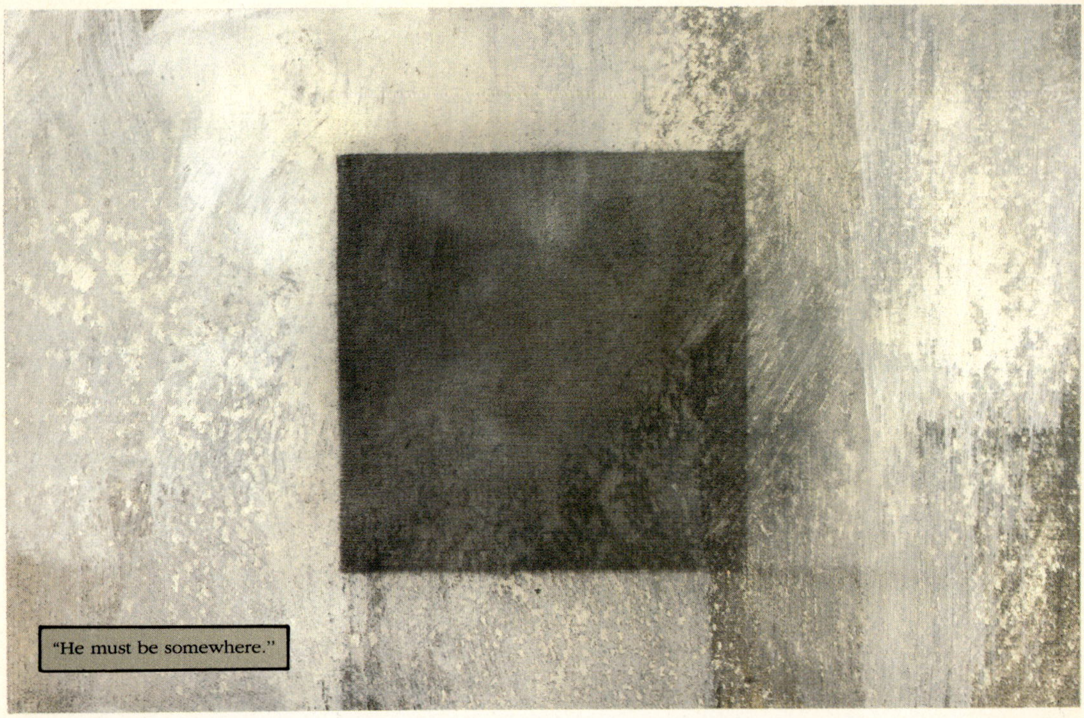
"He must be somewhere."

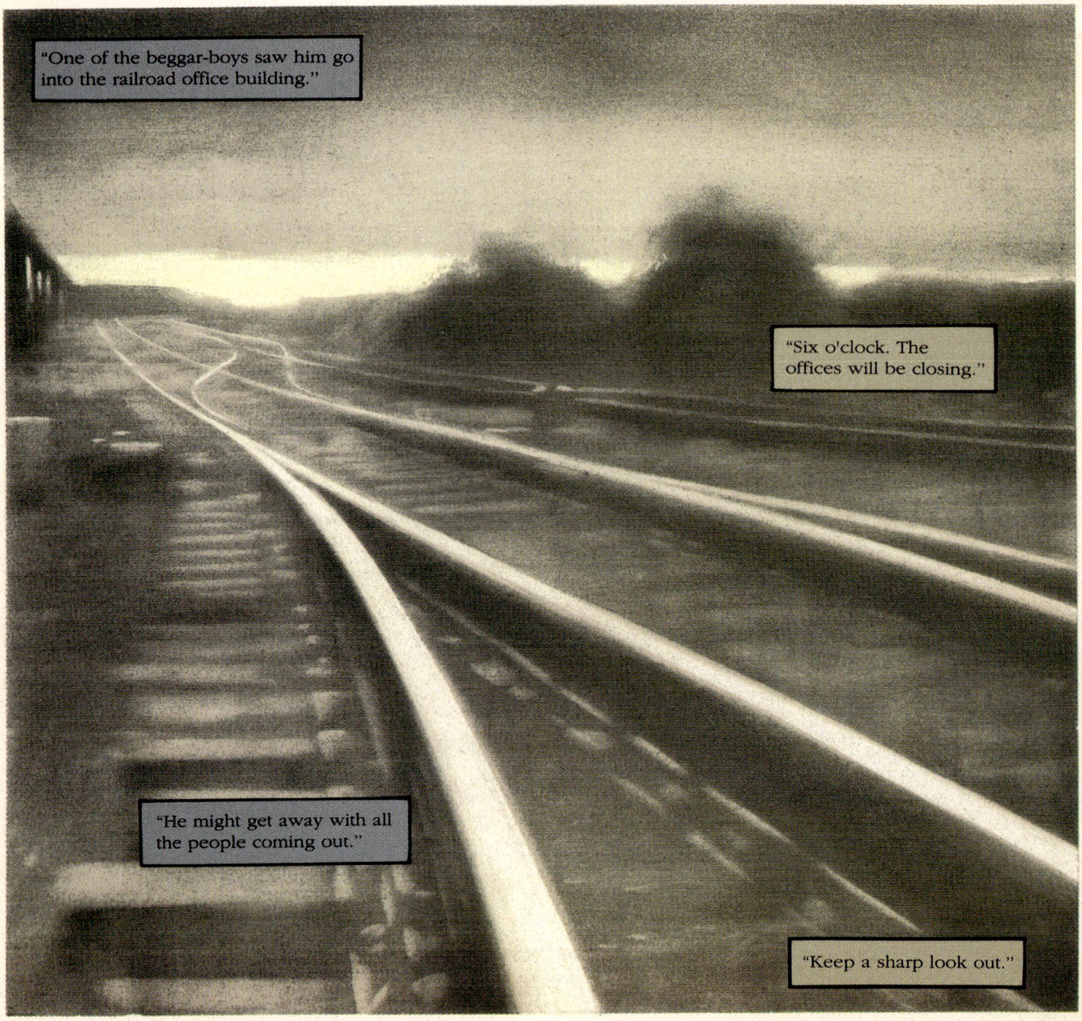
"One of the beggar-boys saw him go into the railroad office building."
"Six o'clock. The offices will be closing."
"He might get away with all the people coming out."
"Keep a sharp look out."

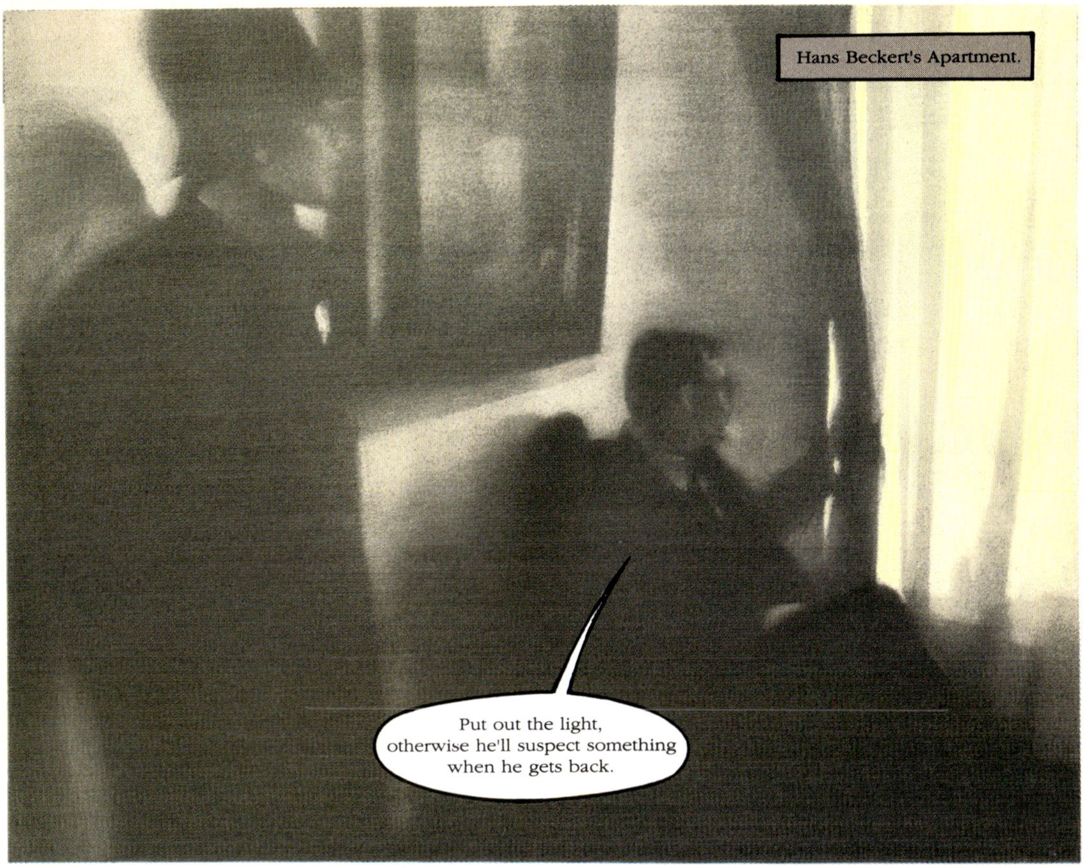
Hans Beckert's Apartment.
Put out the light, otherwise he'll suspect something when he gets back.

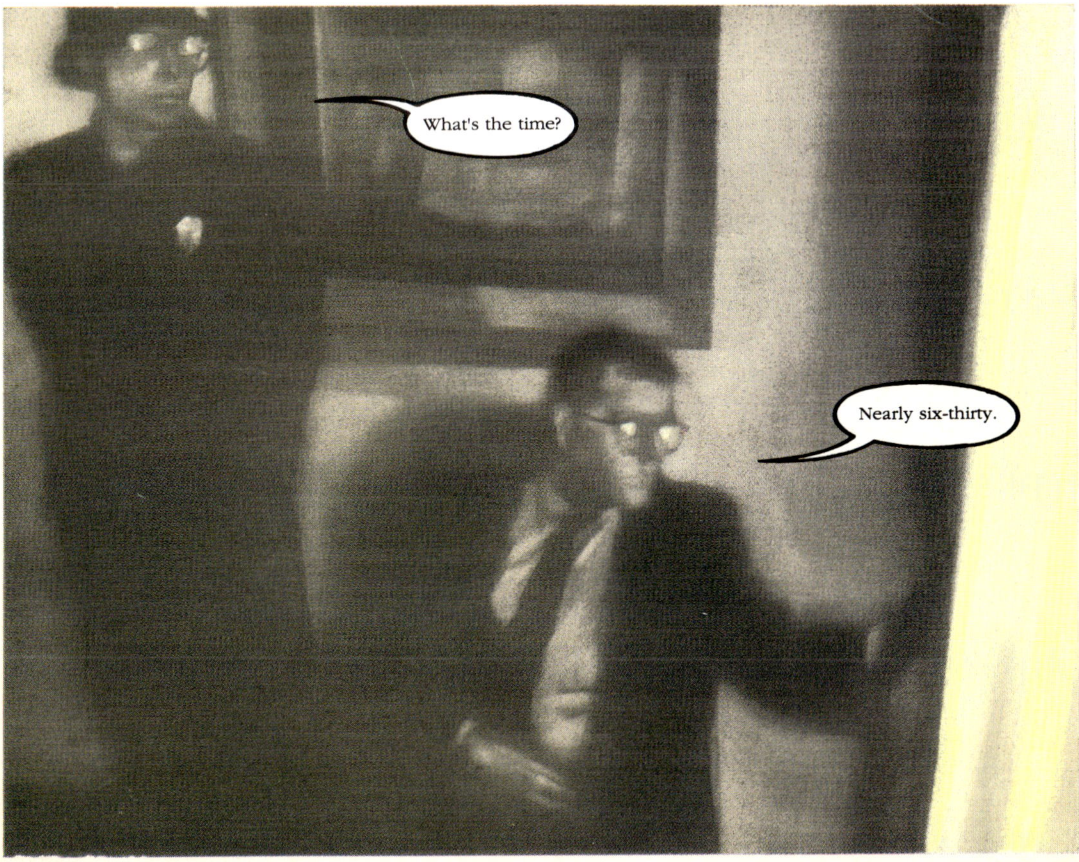
What's the time?
Nearly six-thirty.

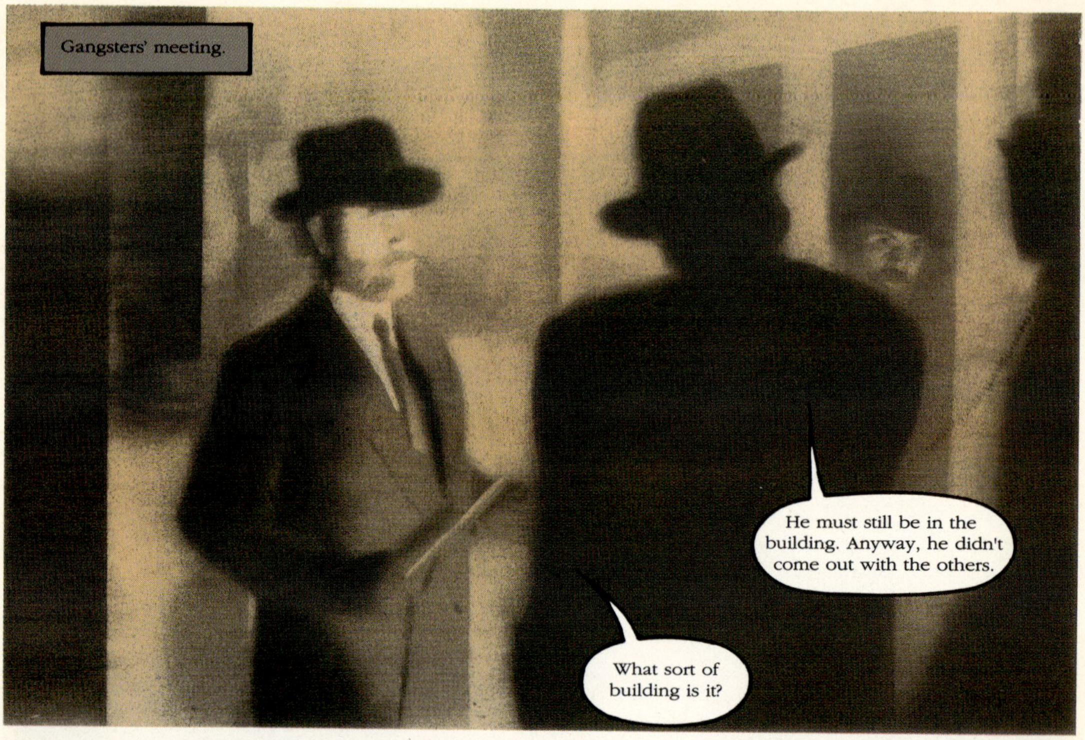
Gangsters' meeting.
He must still be in the building. Anyway, he didn't come out with the others.
What sort of building is it?

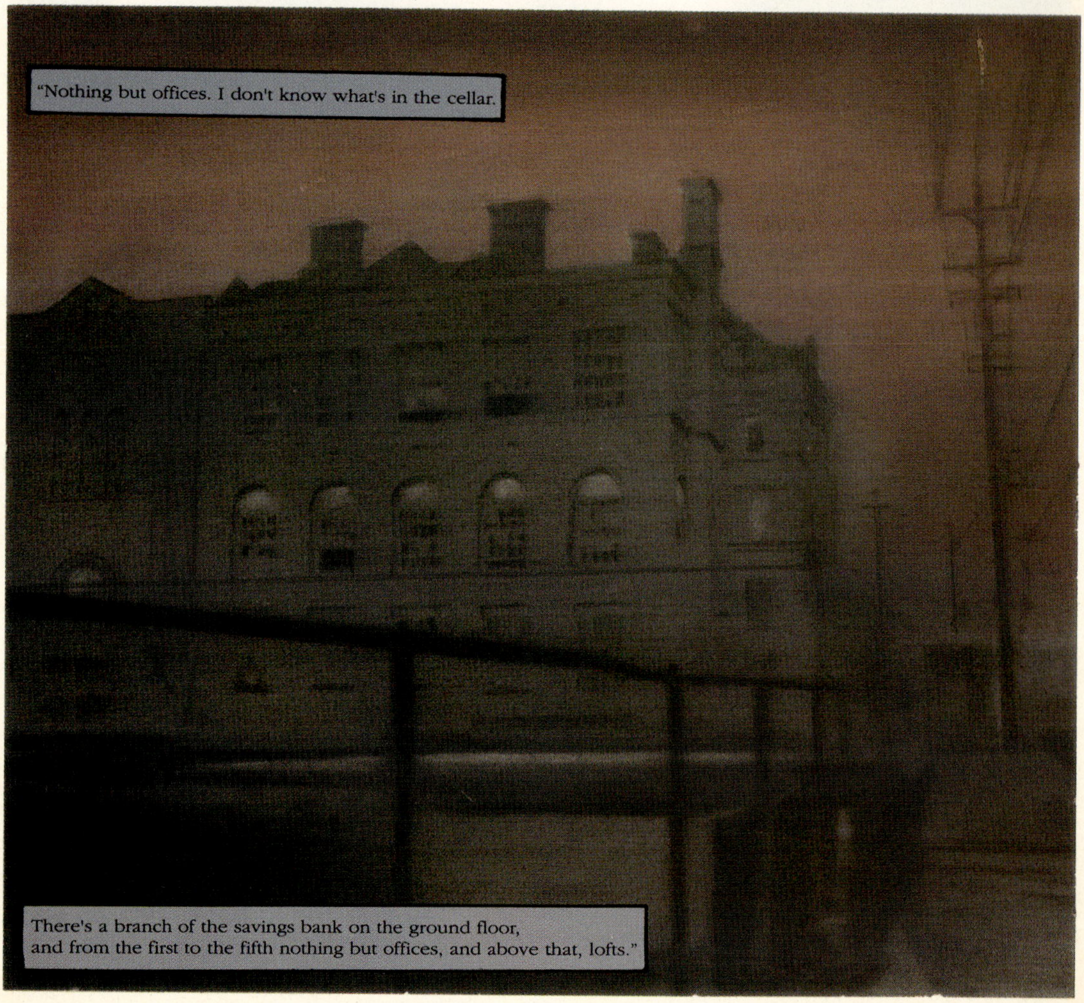
"Nothing but offices. I don't know what's in the cellar.
There's a branch of the savings bank on the ground floor, and from the first to the fifth nothing but offices, and above that, lofts."

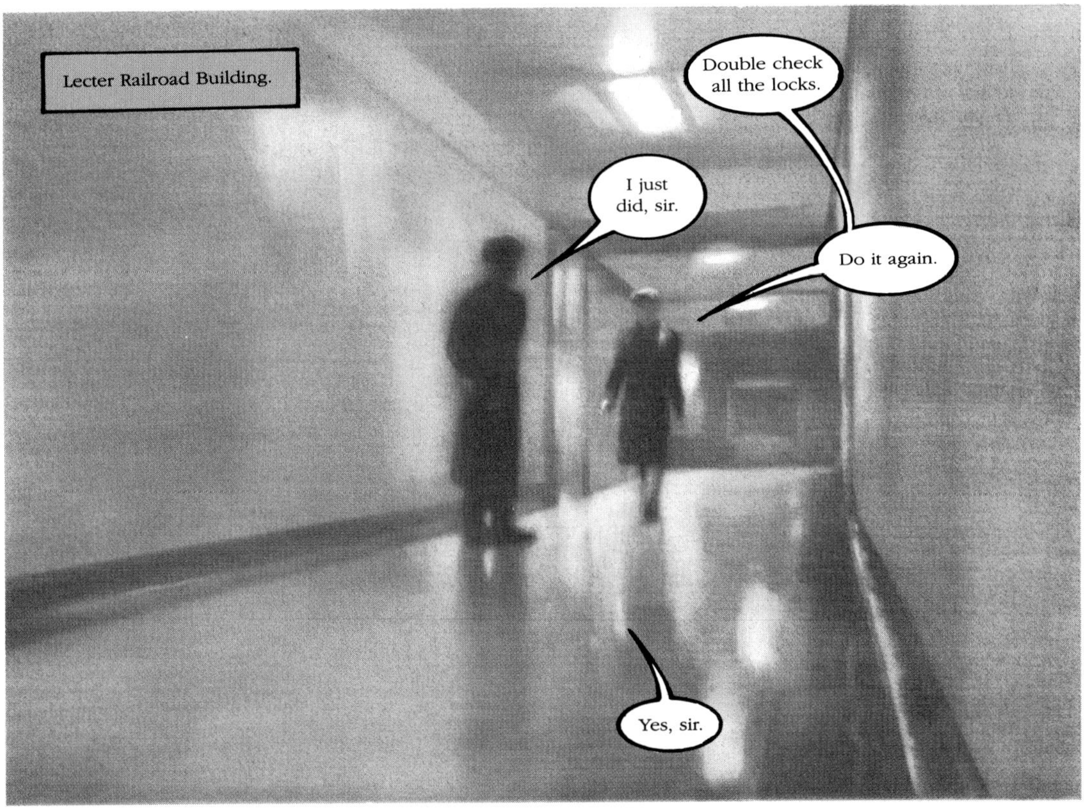
Lecter Railroad Building.
Double check all the locks.
I just did, sir.
Do it again.
Yes, sir.

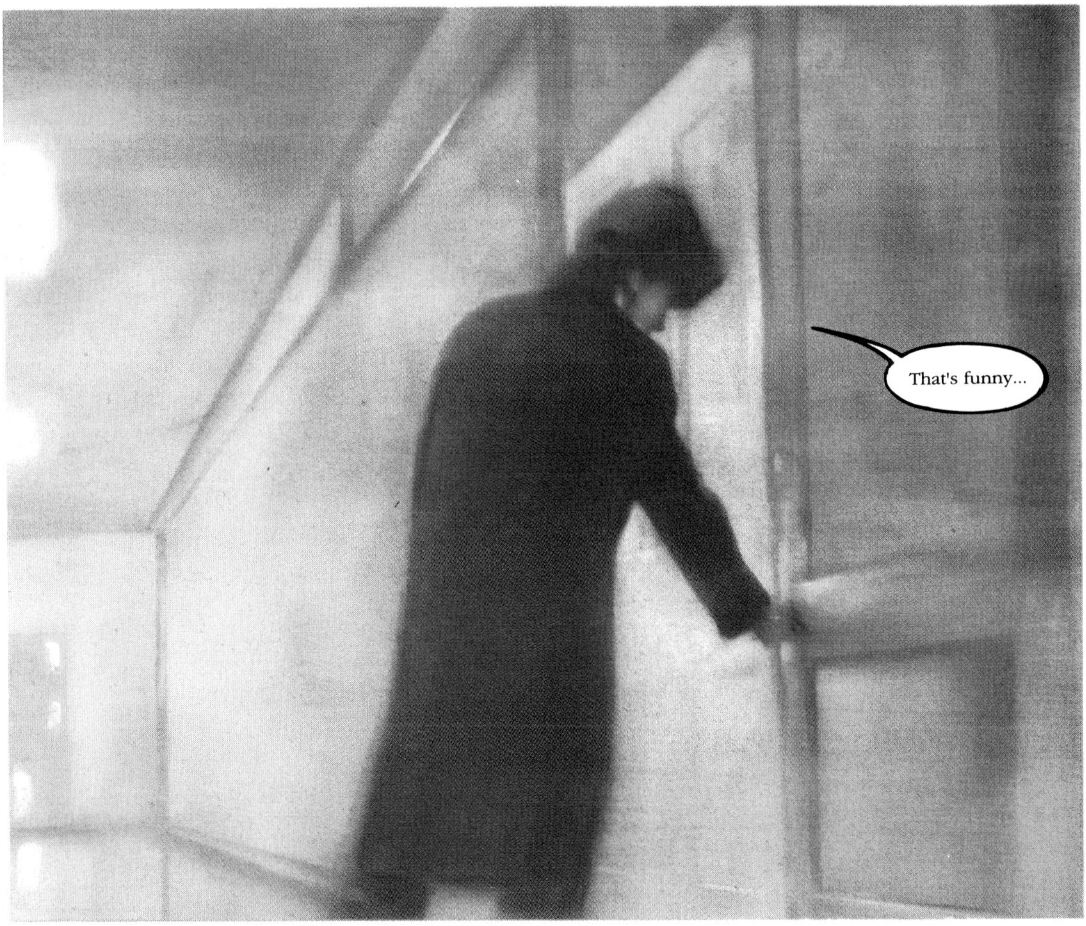
That's funny...

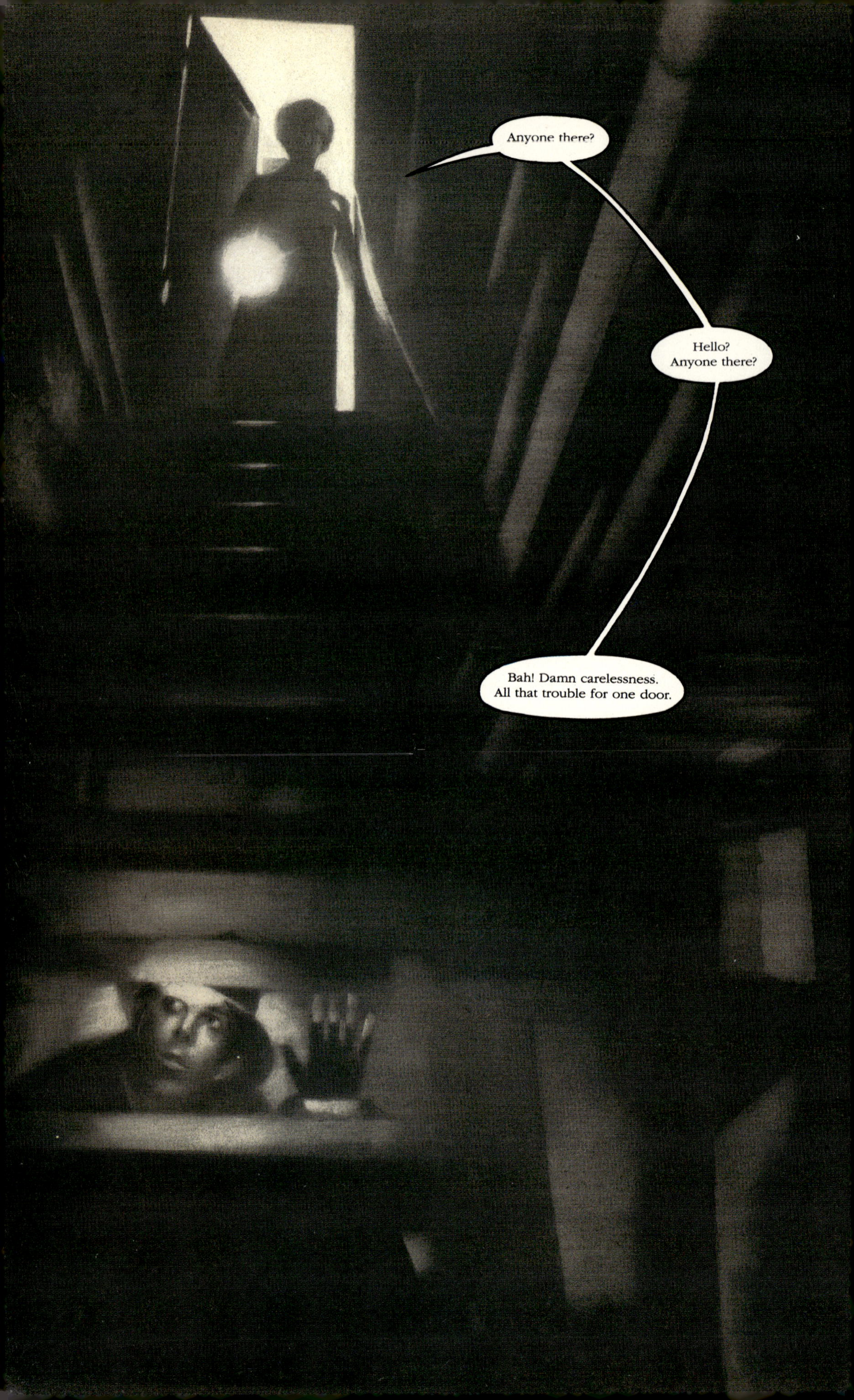
Anyone there?
Hello? Anyone there?
Bah! Damn carelessness. All that trouble for one door.

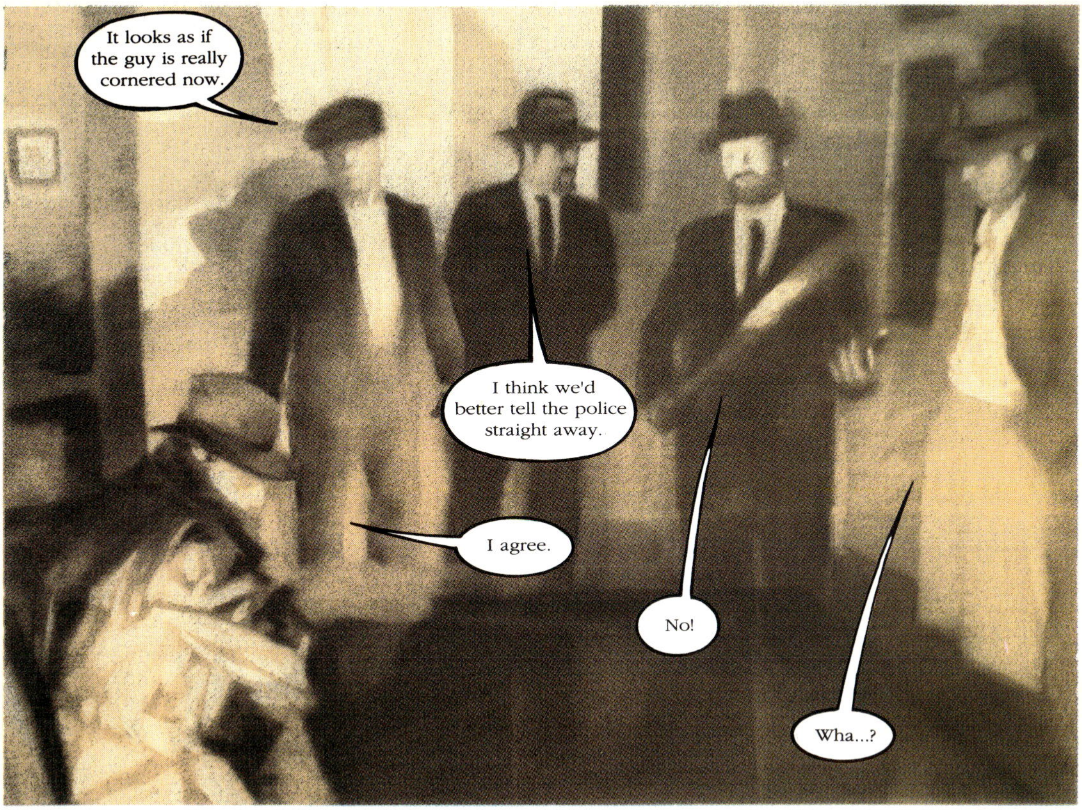
It looks as if the guy is really cornered now.
I think we'd better tell the police straight away.
I agree.
No!
Wha...?
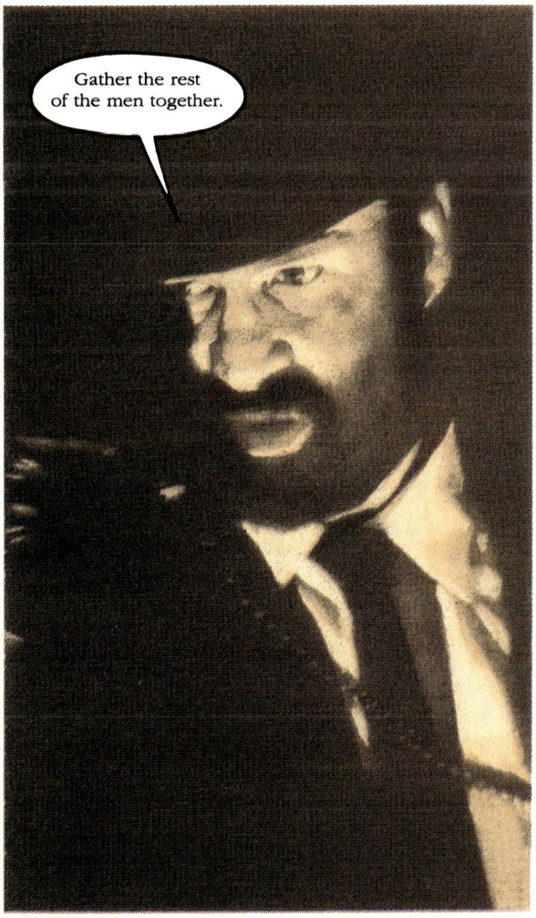
Gather the rest of the men together.
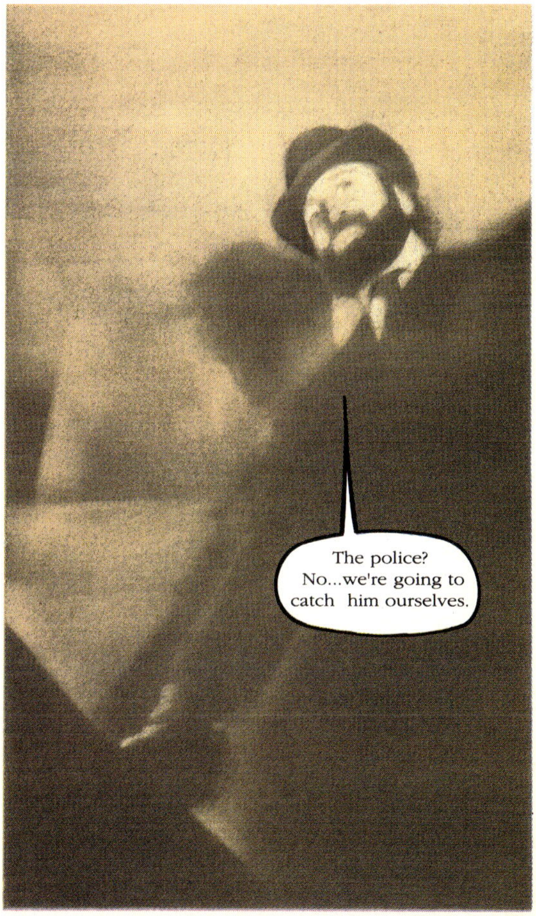
The police? No...we're going to catch him ourselves.

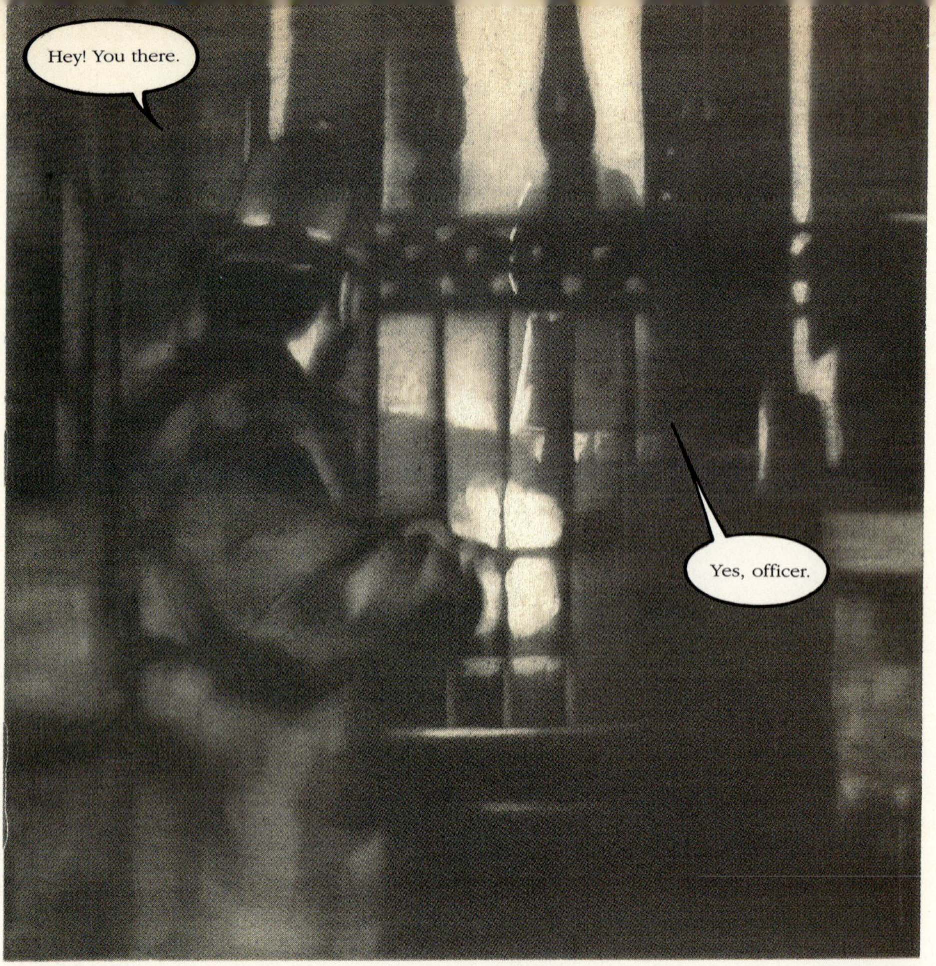
Hey! You there.
Yes, officer.

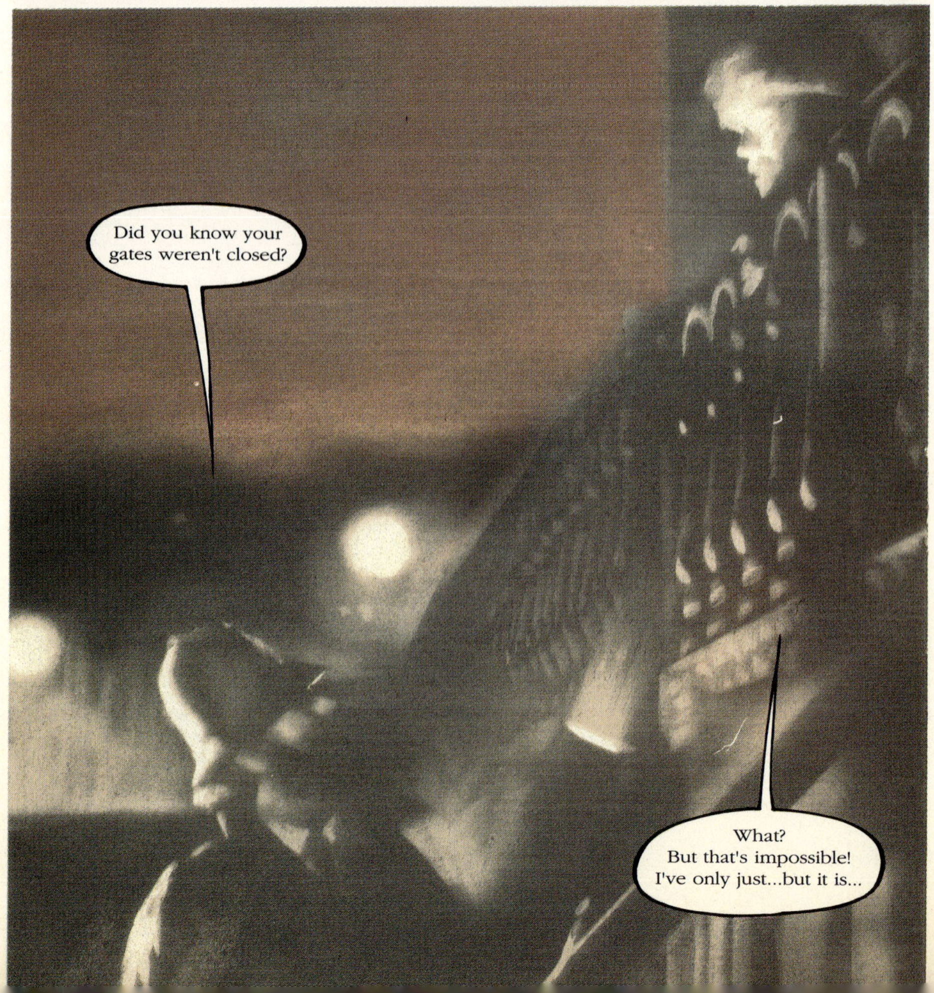
Did you know your gates weren't closed?
What? But that's impossible! I've only just...but it is...

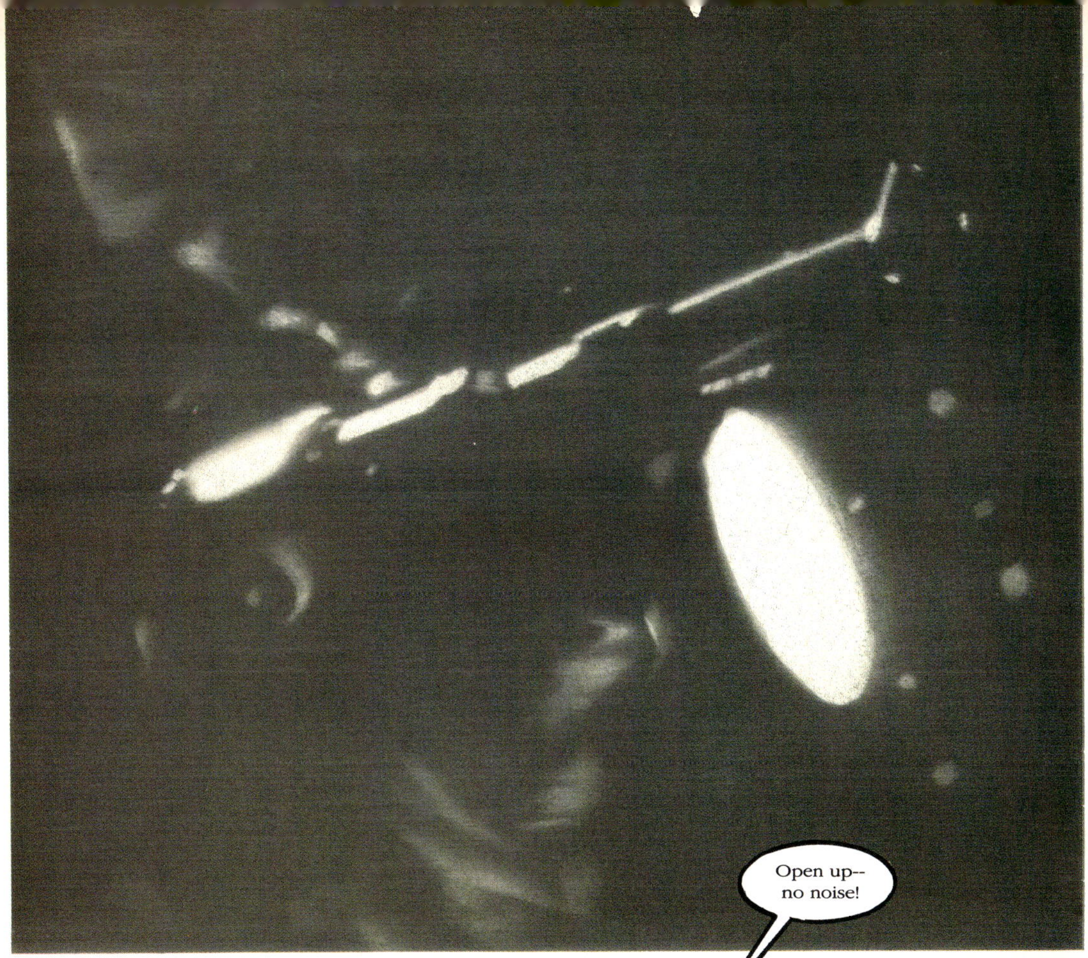

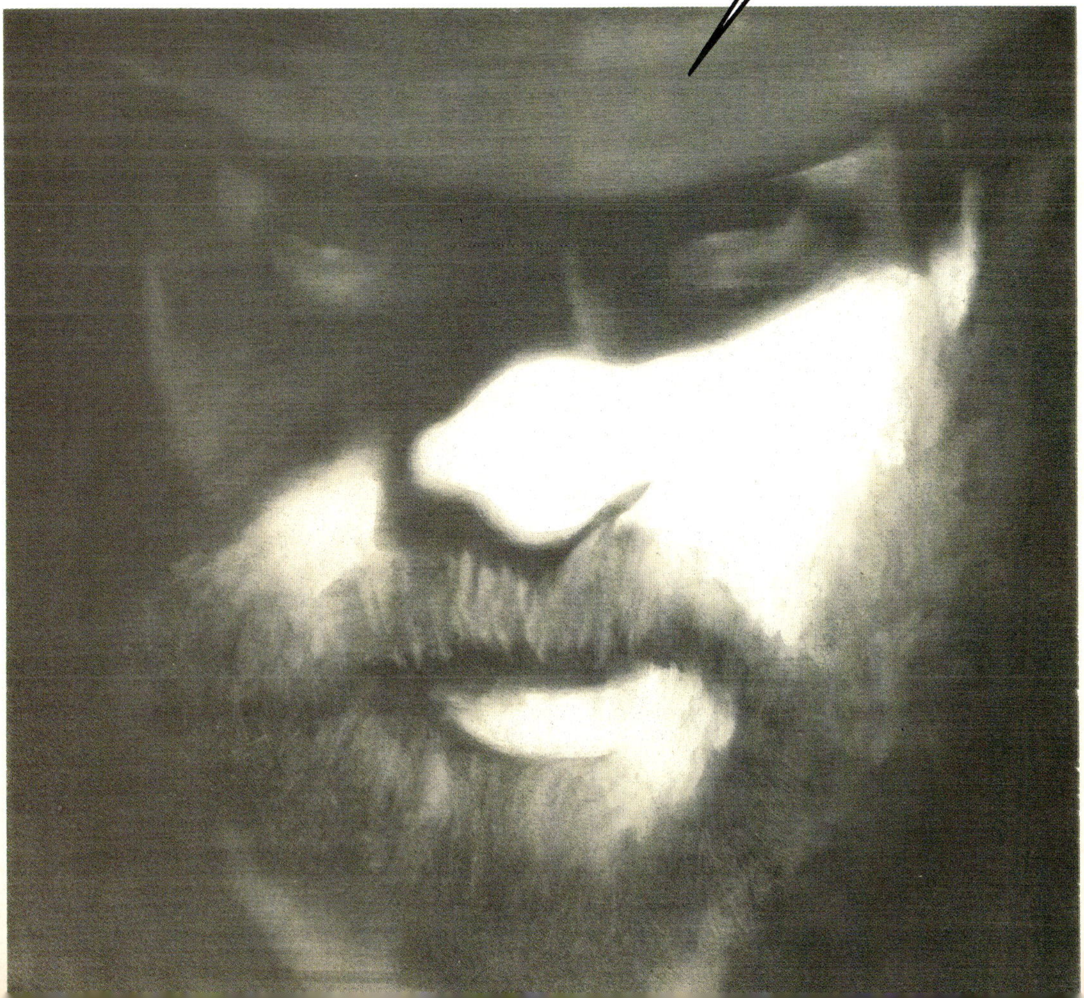
Open up--
no noise!

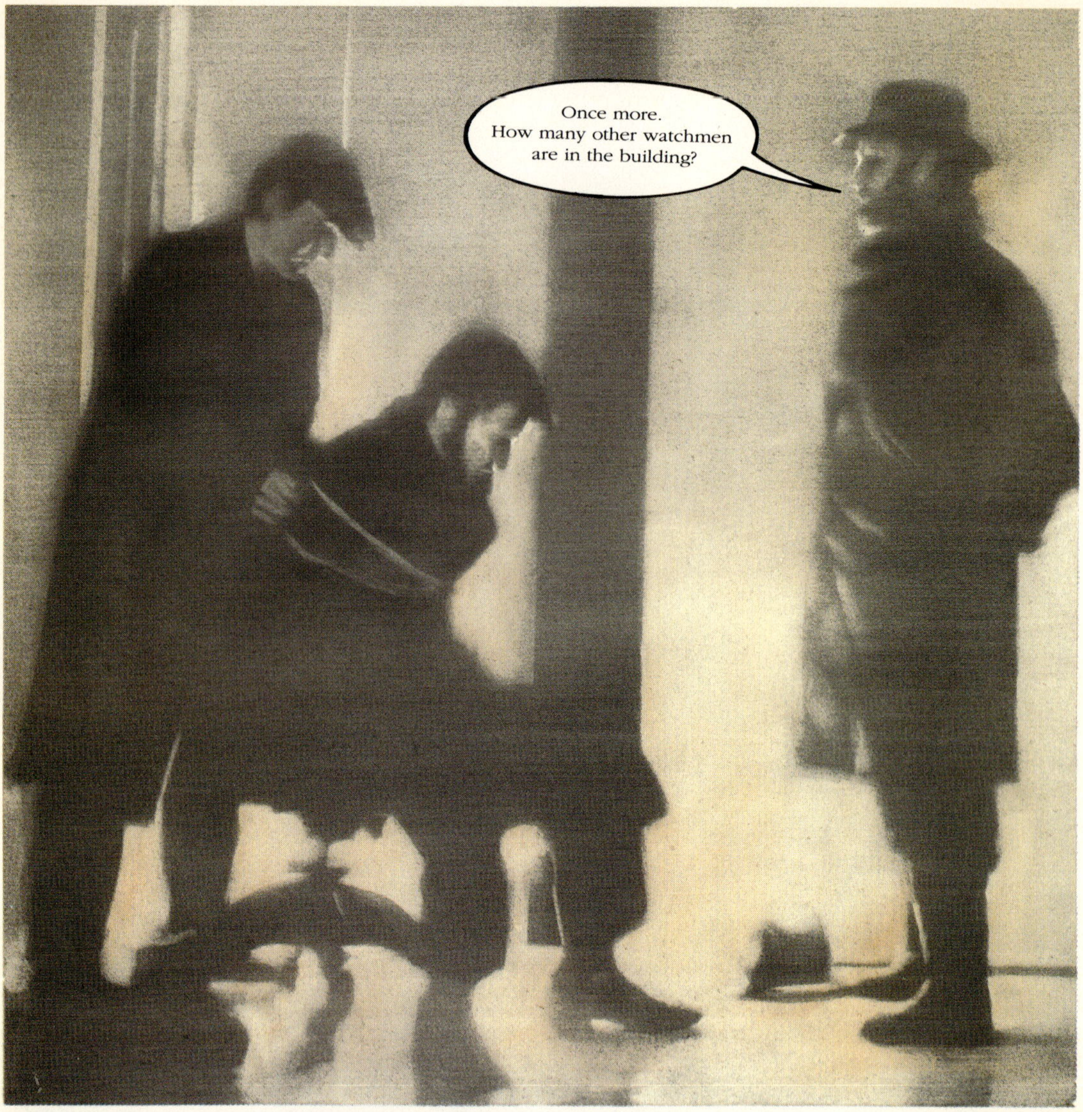
Once more.
How many other watchmen
are in the building?

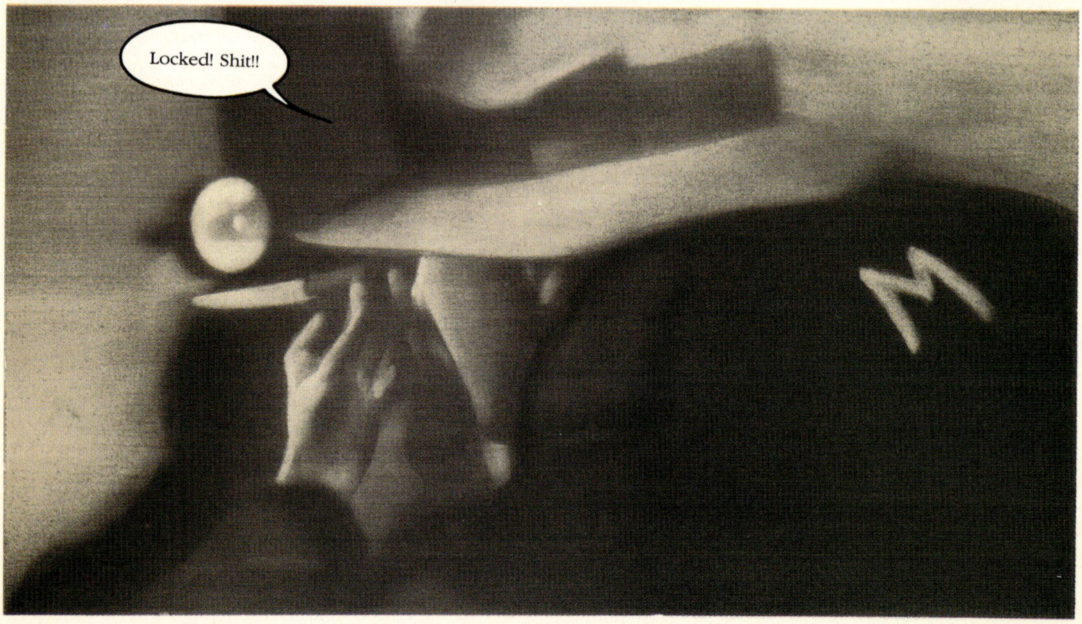
Locked! Shit!!

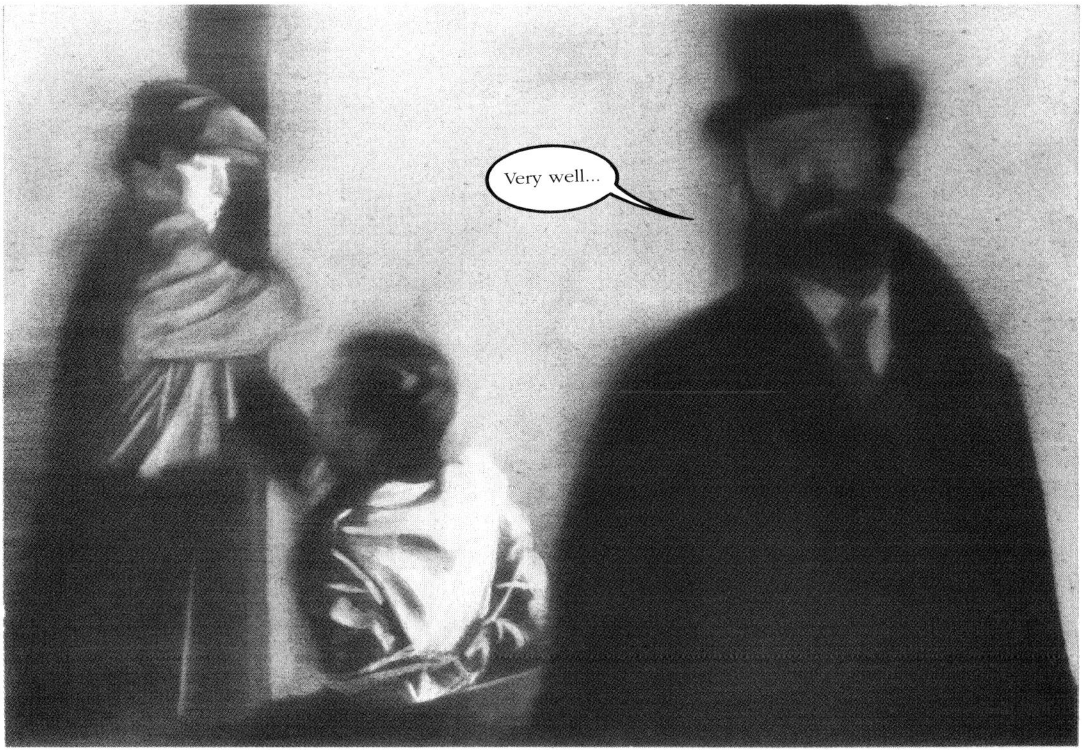
Very well...

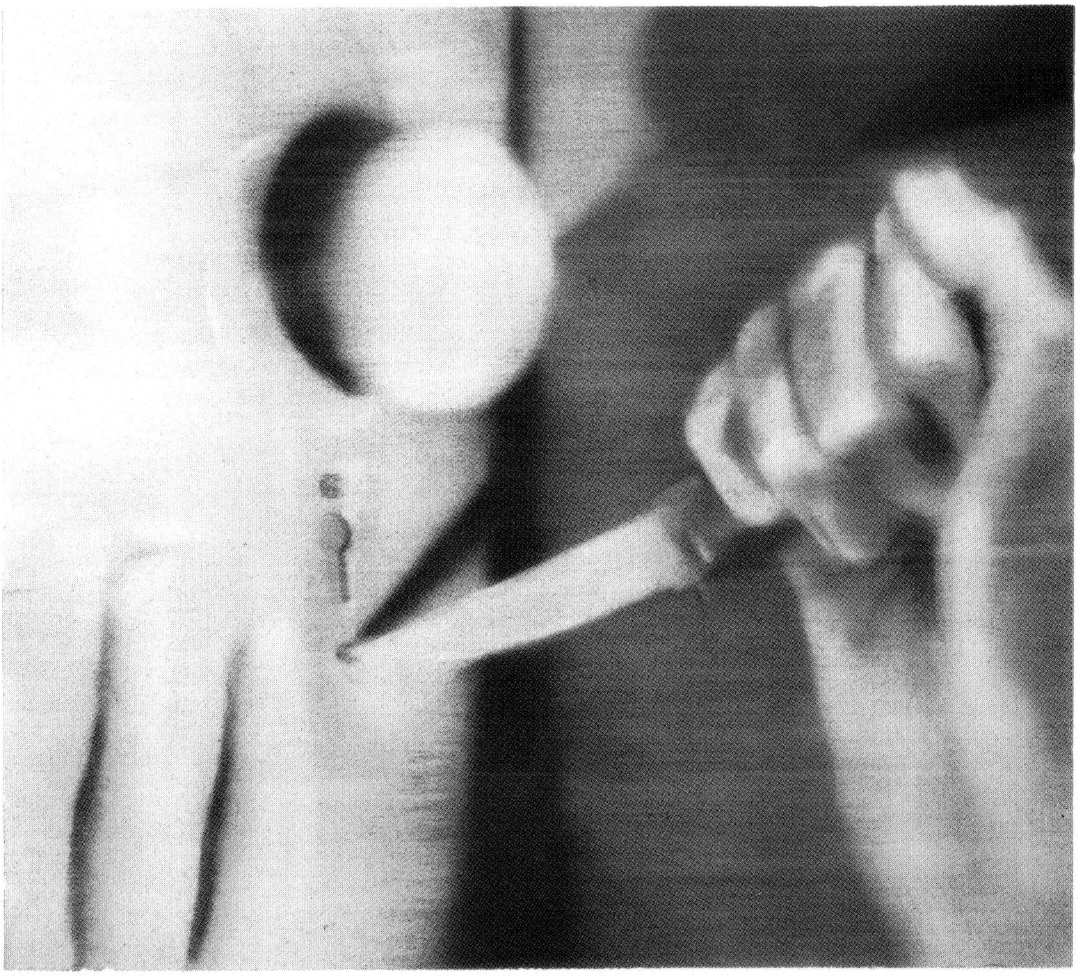

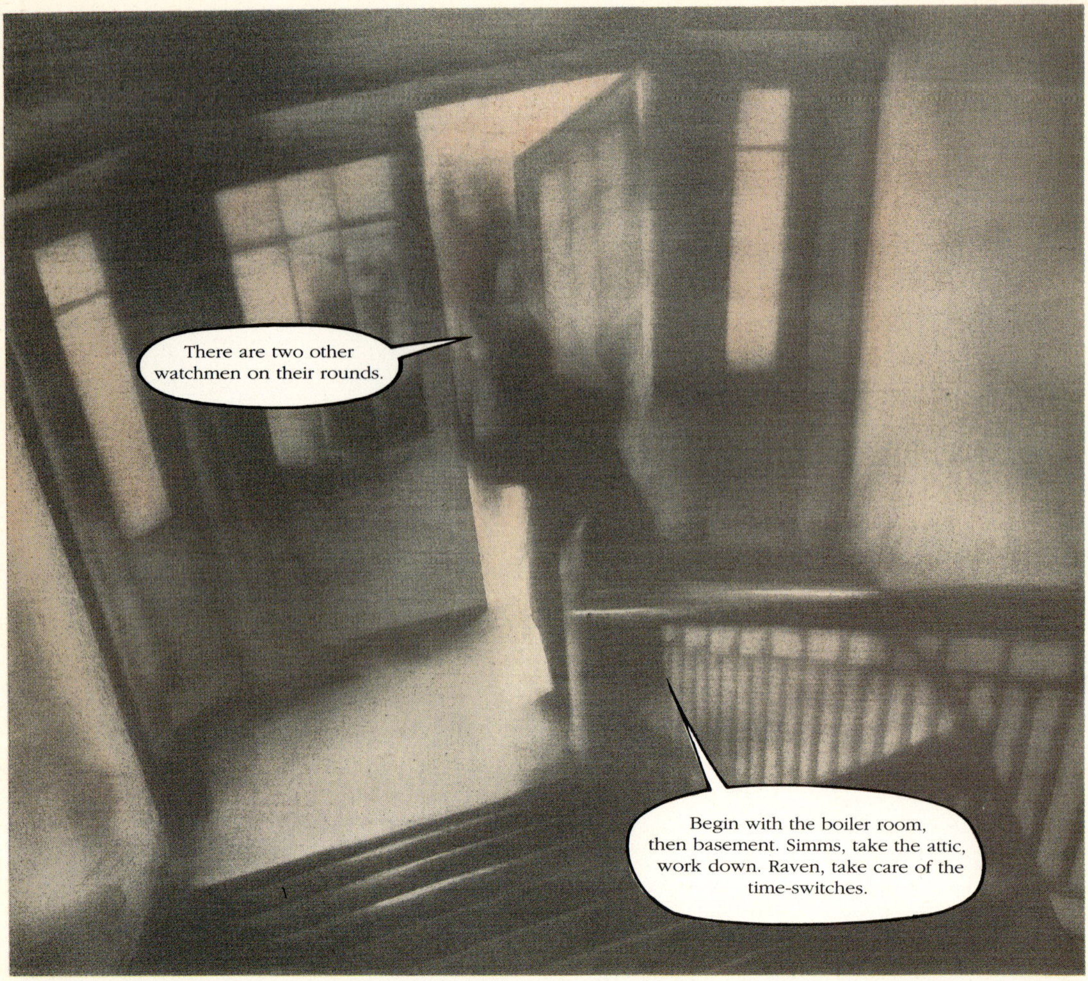
There are two other watchmen on their rounds.
Begin with the boiler room, then basement. Simms, take the attic, work down. Raven, take care of the time-switches.

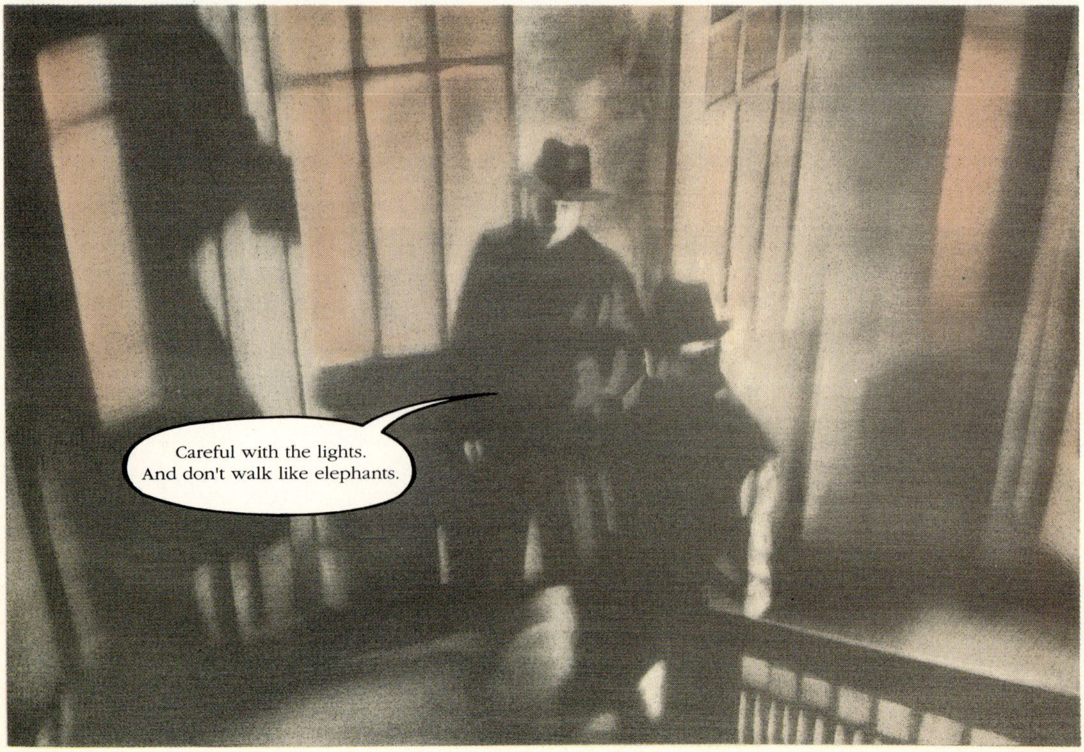
Careful with the lights. And don't walk like elephants.

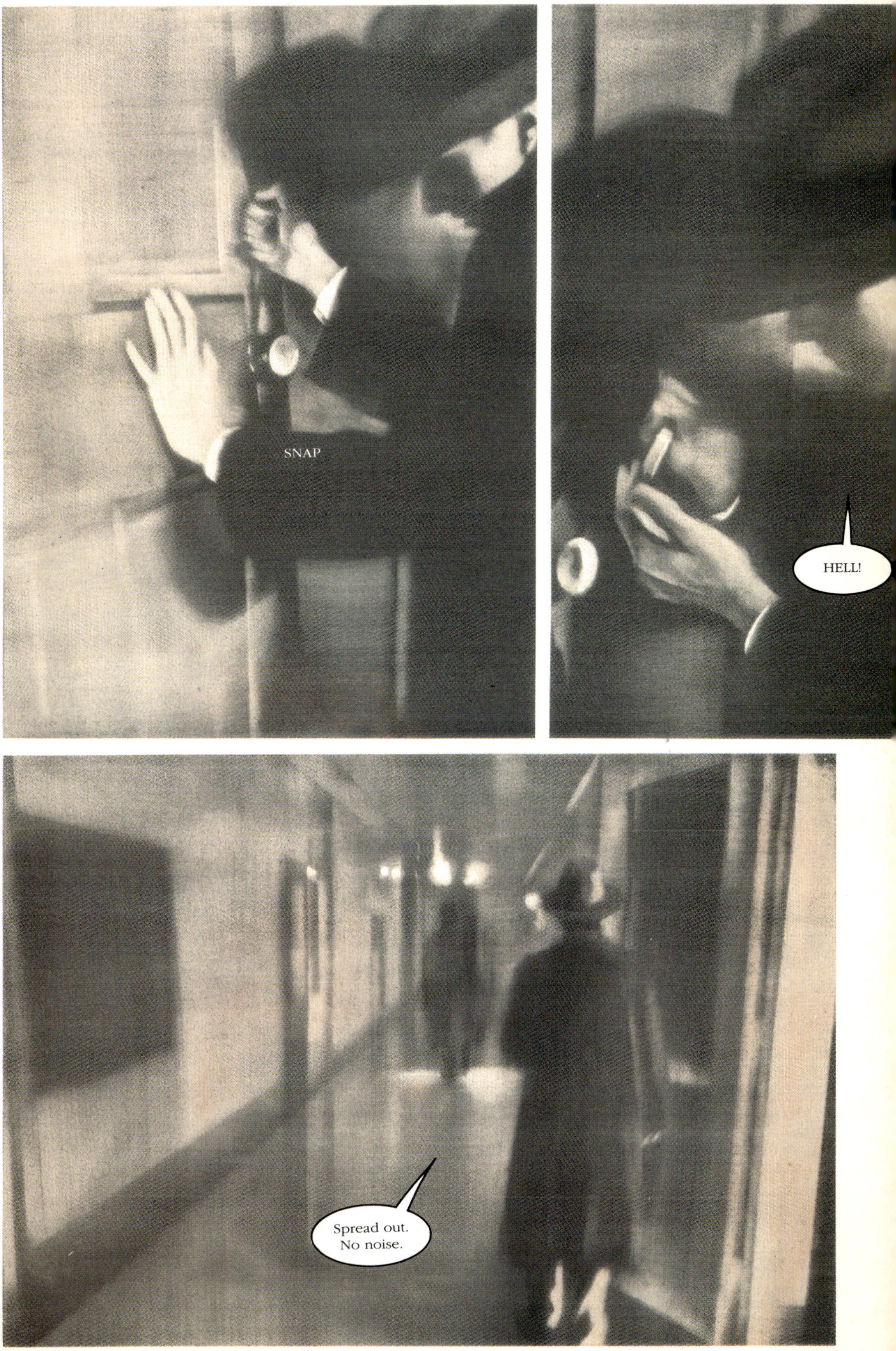
SNAP
HELL!
Spread out. No noise.

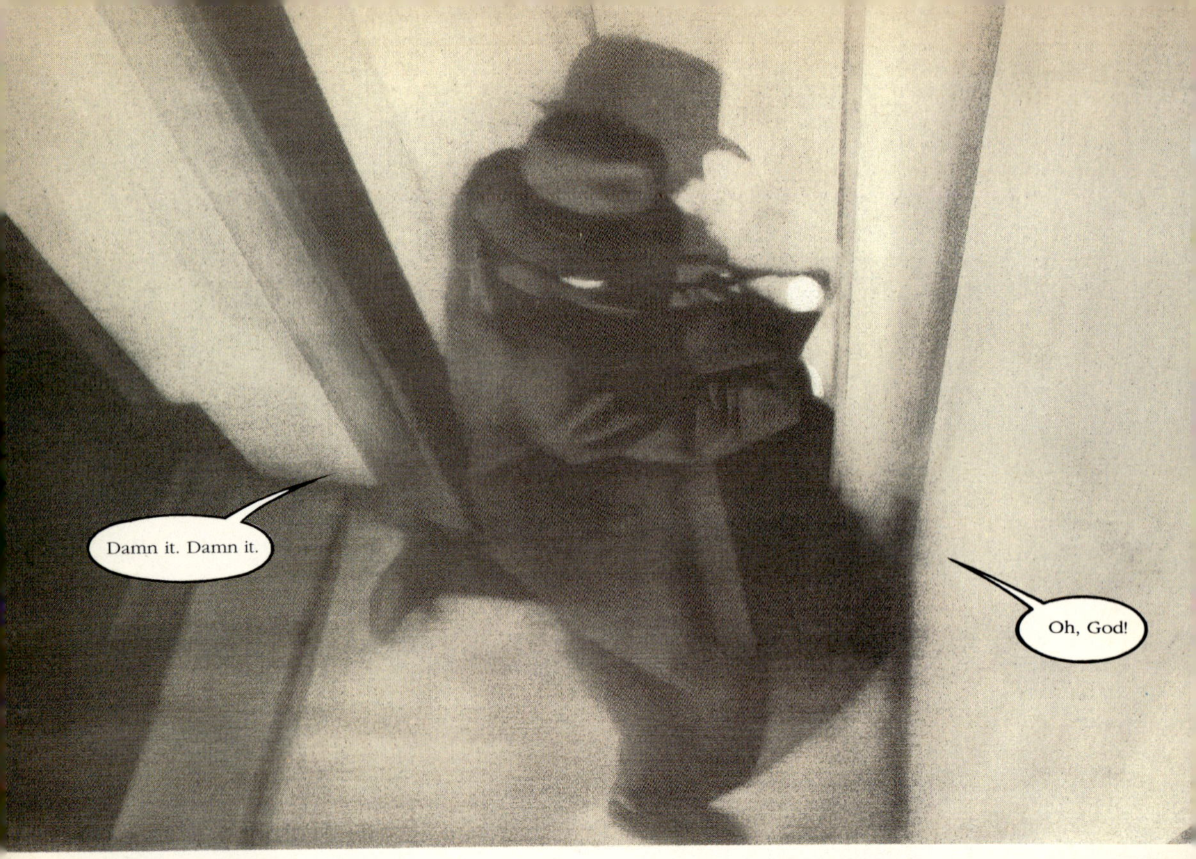
Damn it. Damn it.
Oh, God!

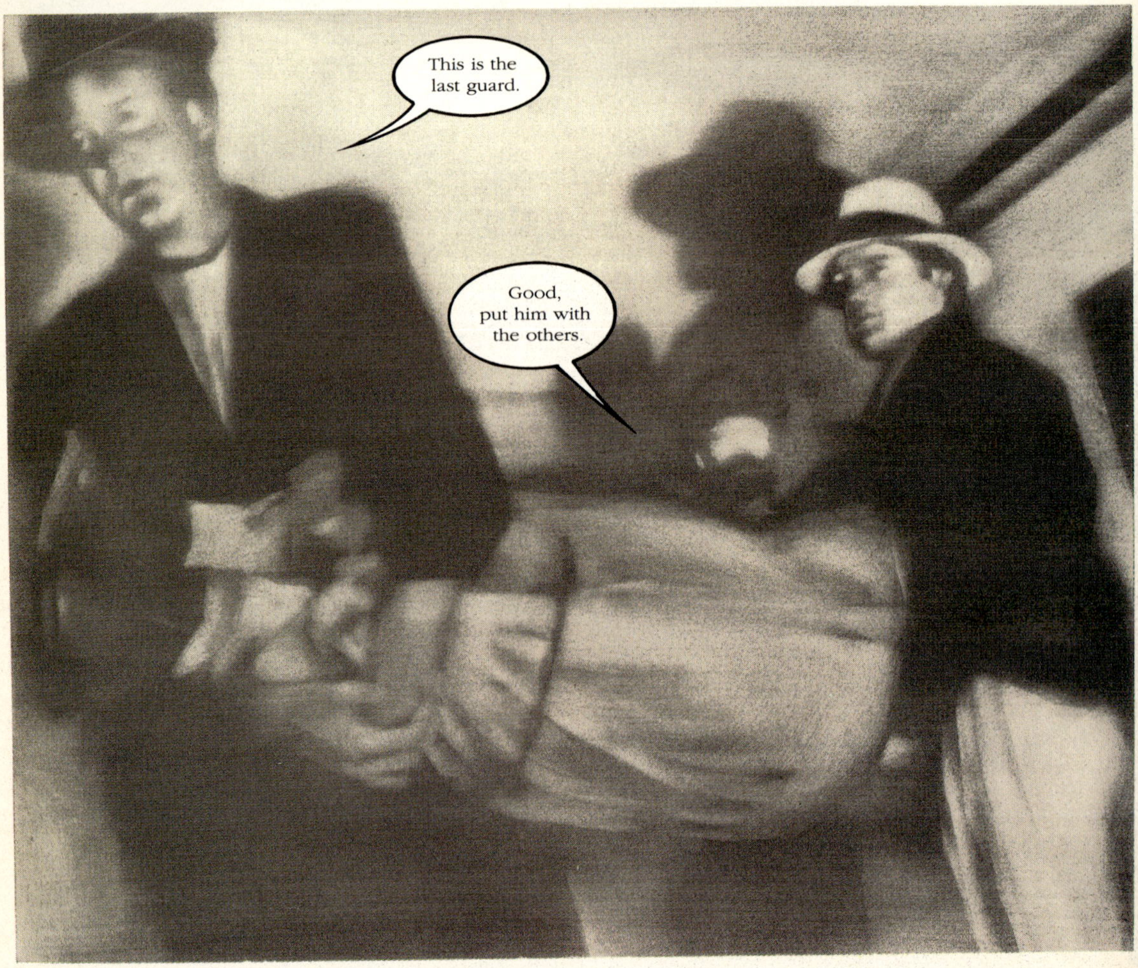
This is the last guard.
Good, put him with the others.

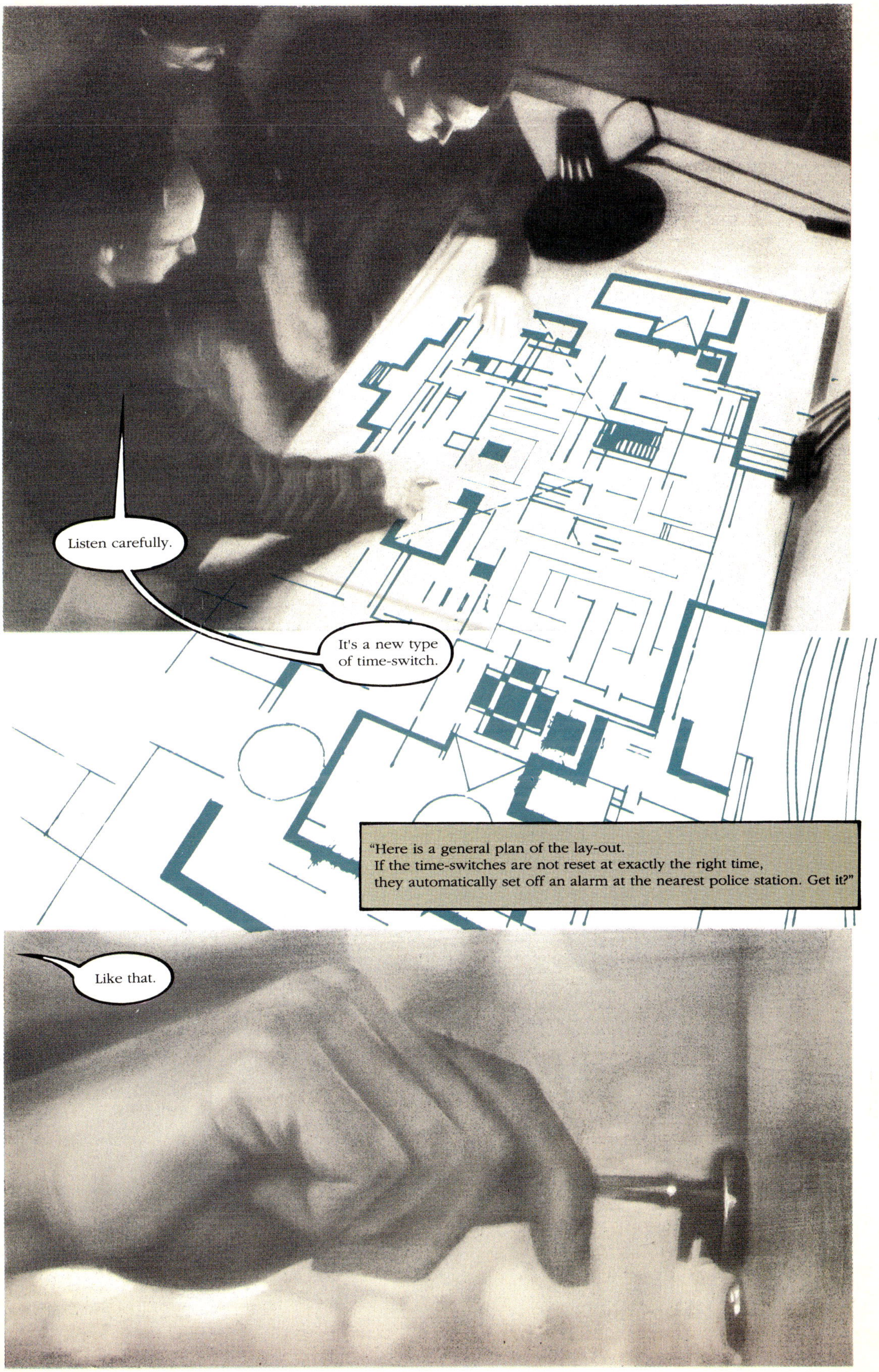
Listen carefully.
It's a new type of time-switch.
"Here is a general plan of the lay-out. If the time-switches are not reset at exactly the right time, they automatically set off an alarm at the nearest police station. Get it?"
Like that.

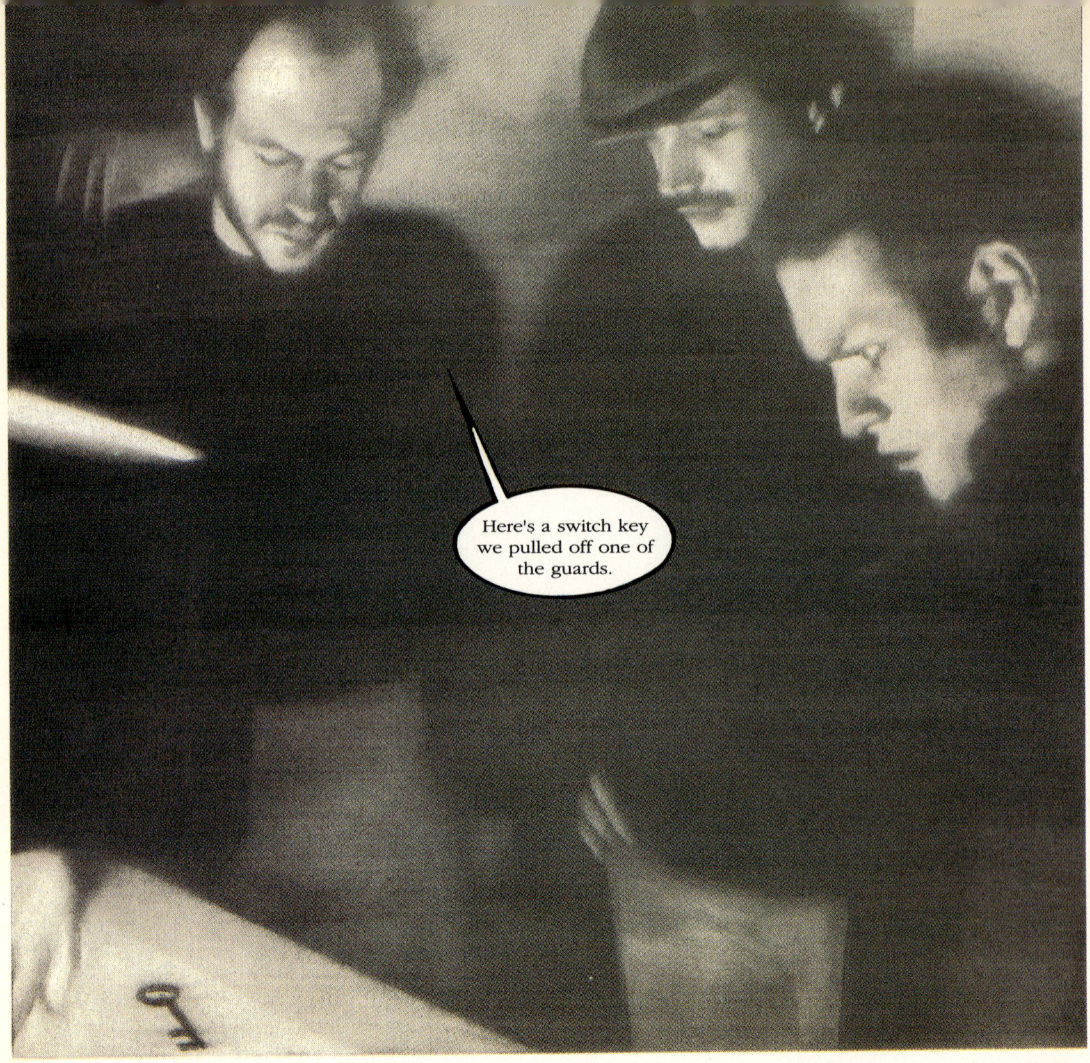
Here's a switch key we pulled off one of the guards.

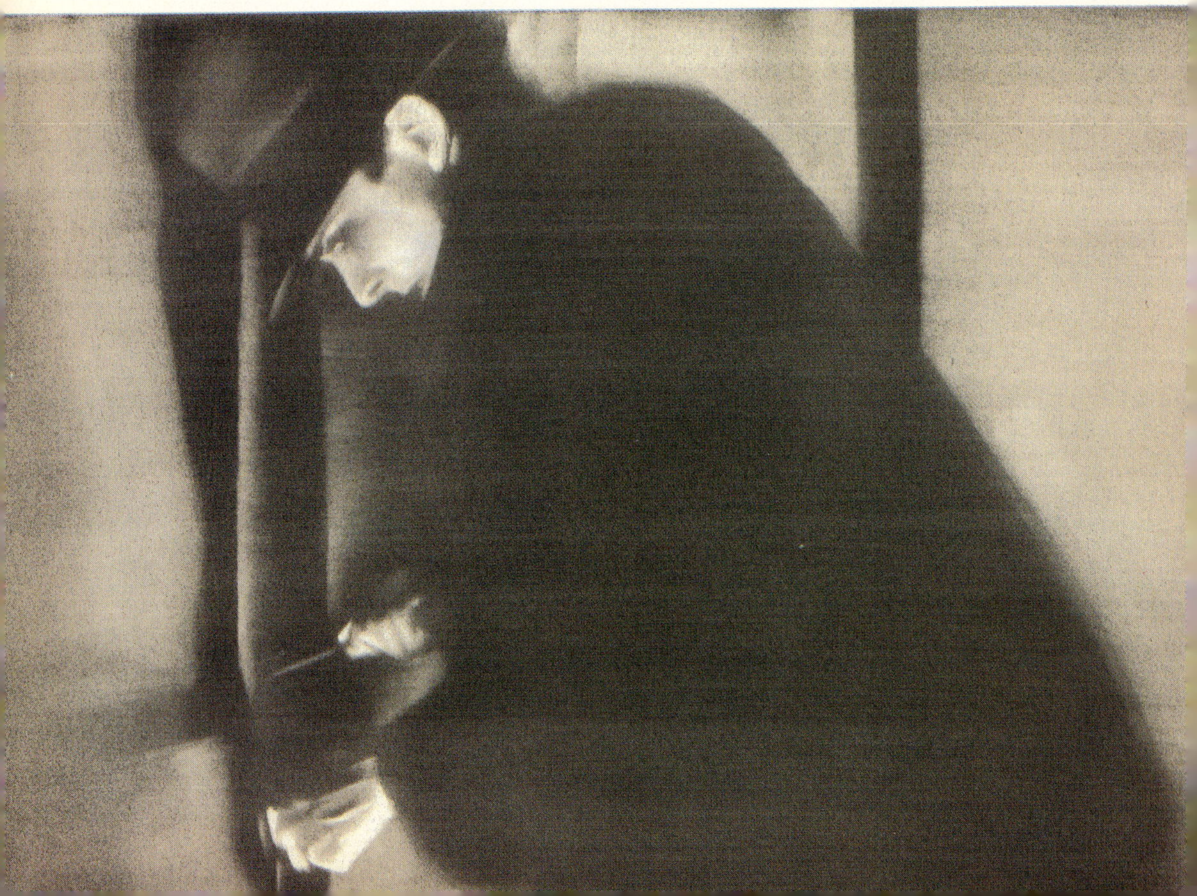

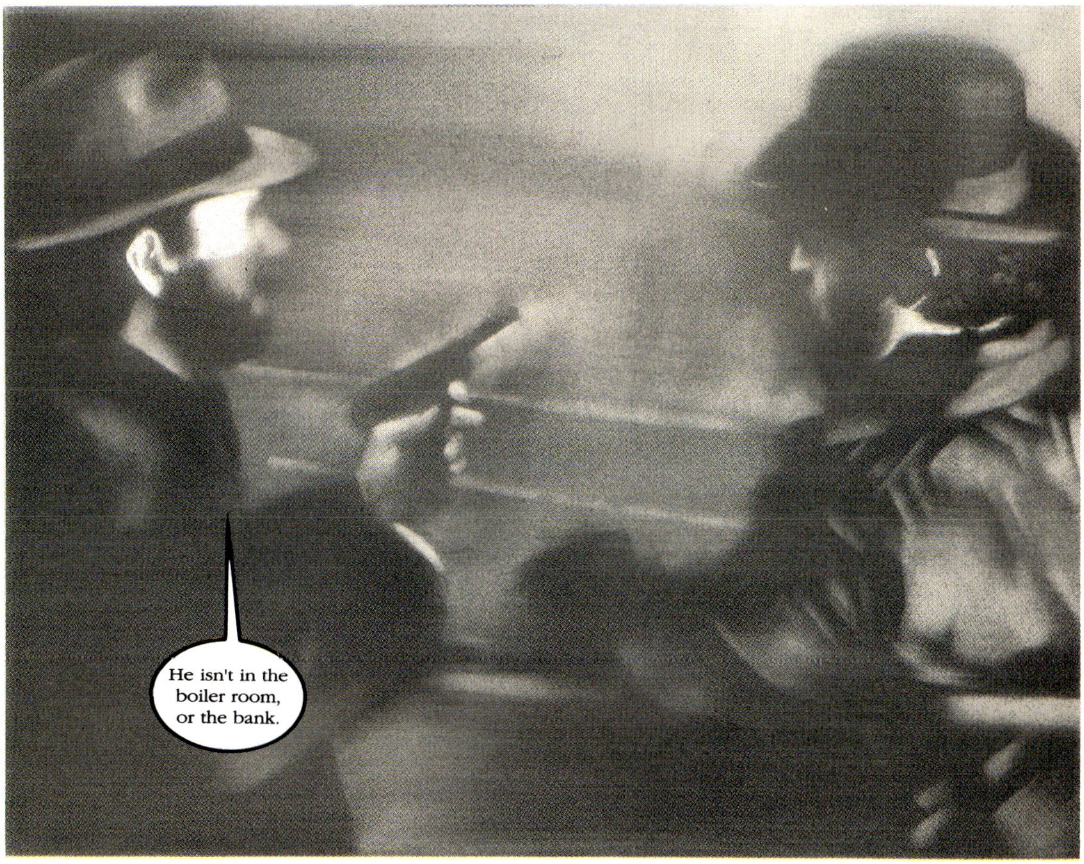
He isn't in the boiler room, or the bank.

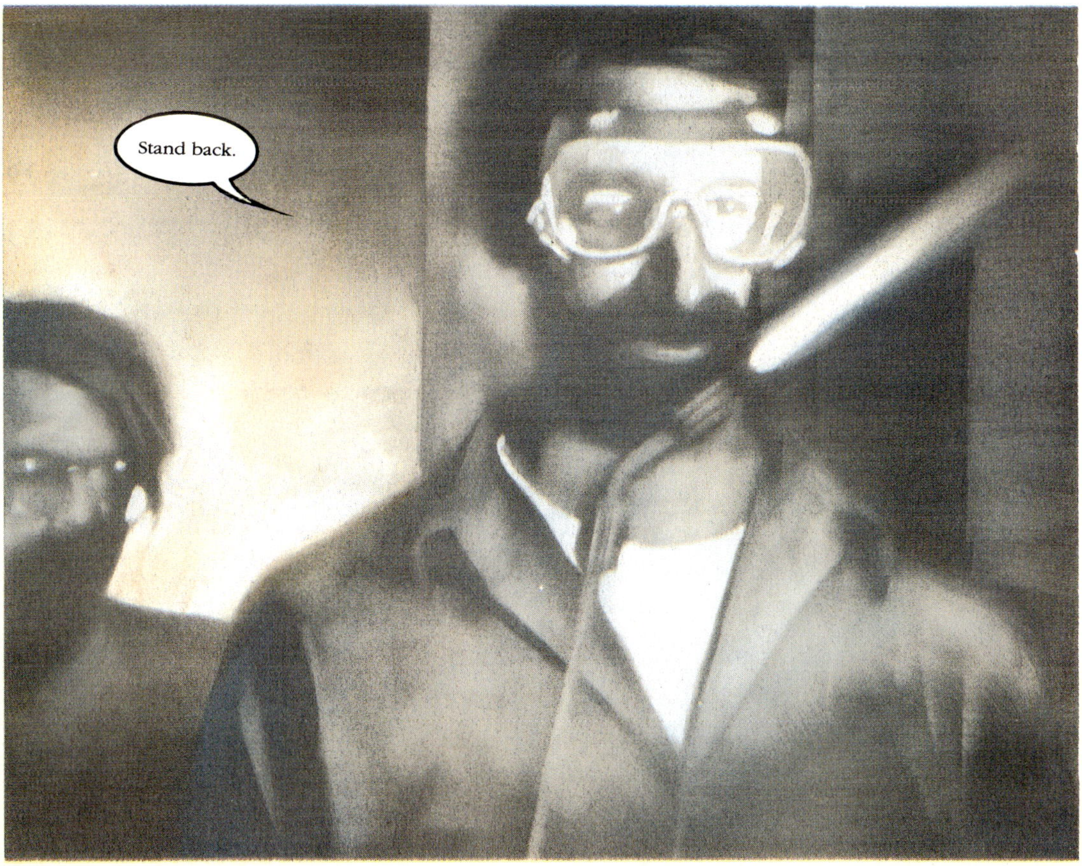
Stand back.

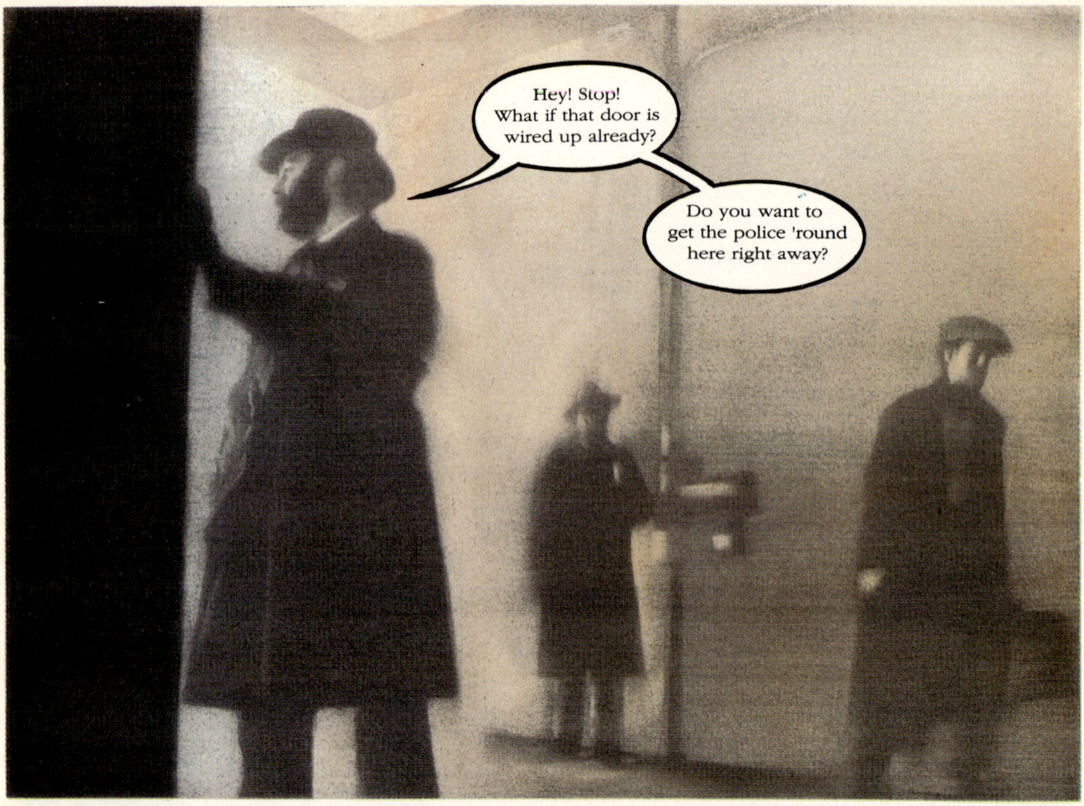
Hey! Stop!
What if that door is
wired up already?
Do you want to
get the police 'round
here right away?

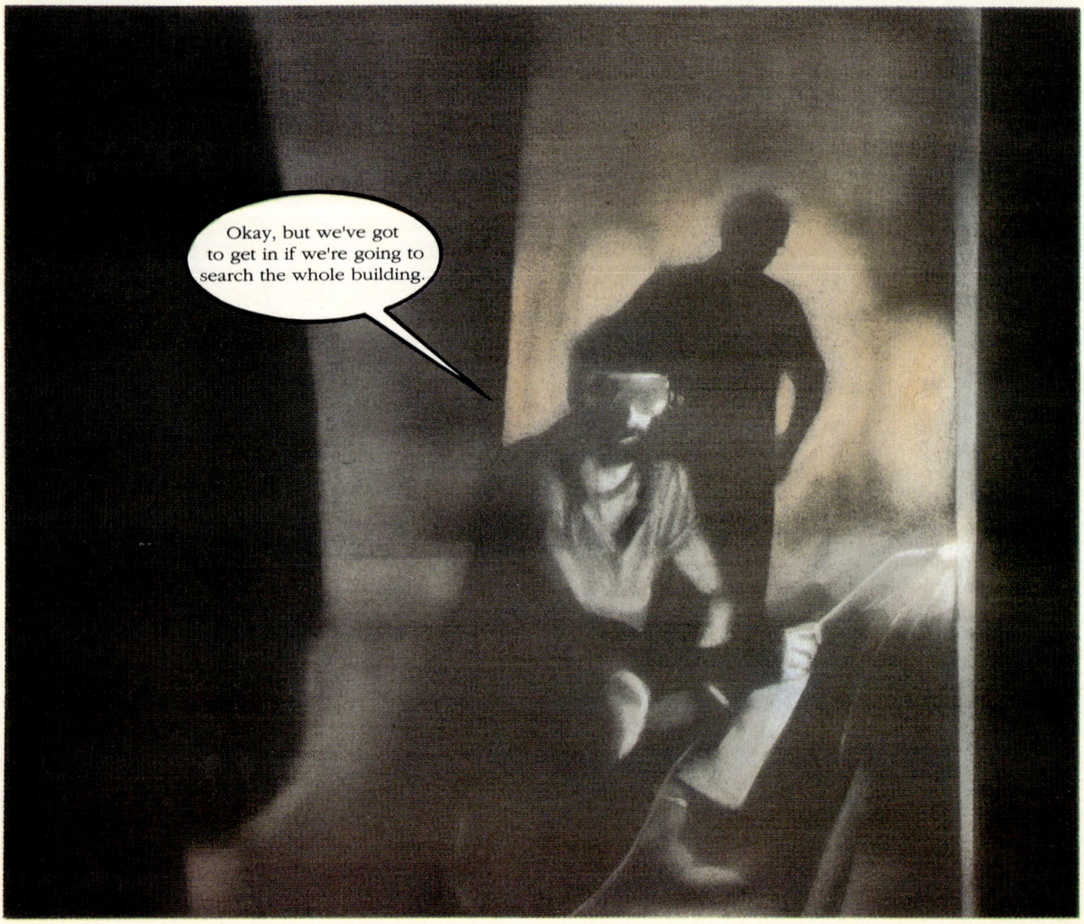
Okay, but we've got
to get in if we're going to
search the whole building.

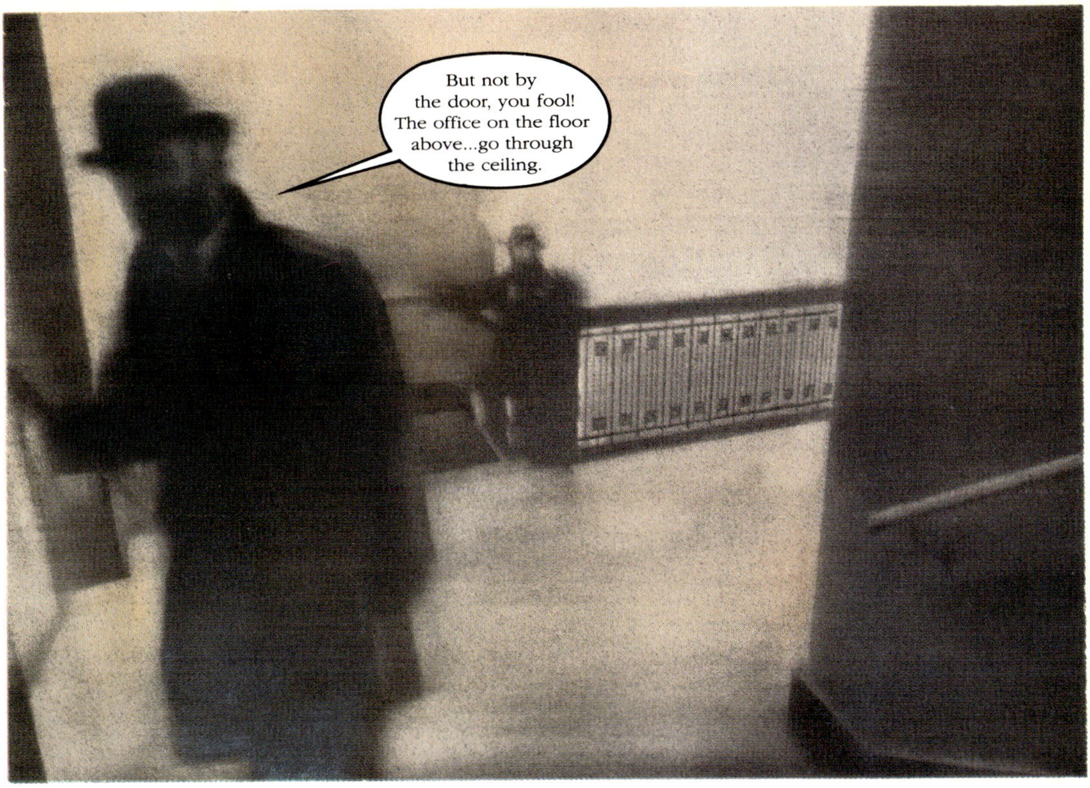
But not by the door, you fool! The office on the floor above...go through the ceiling.

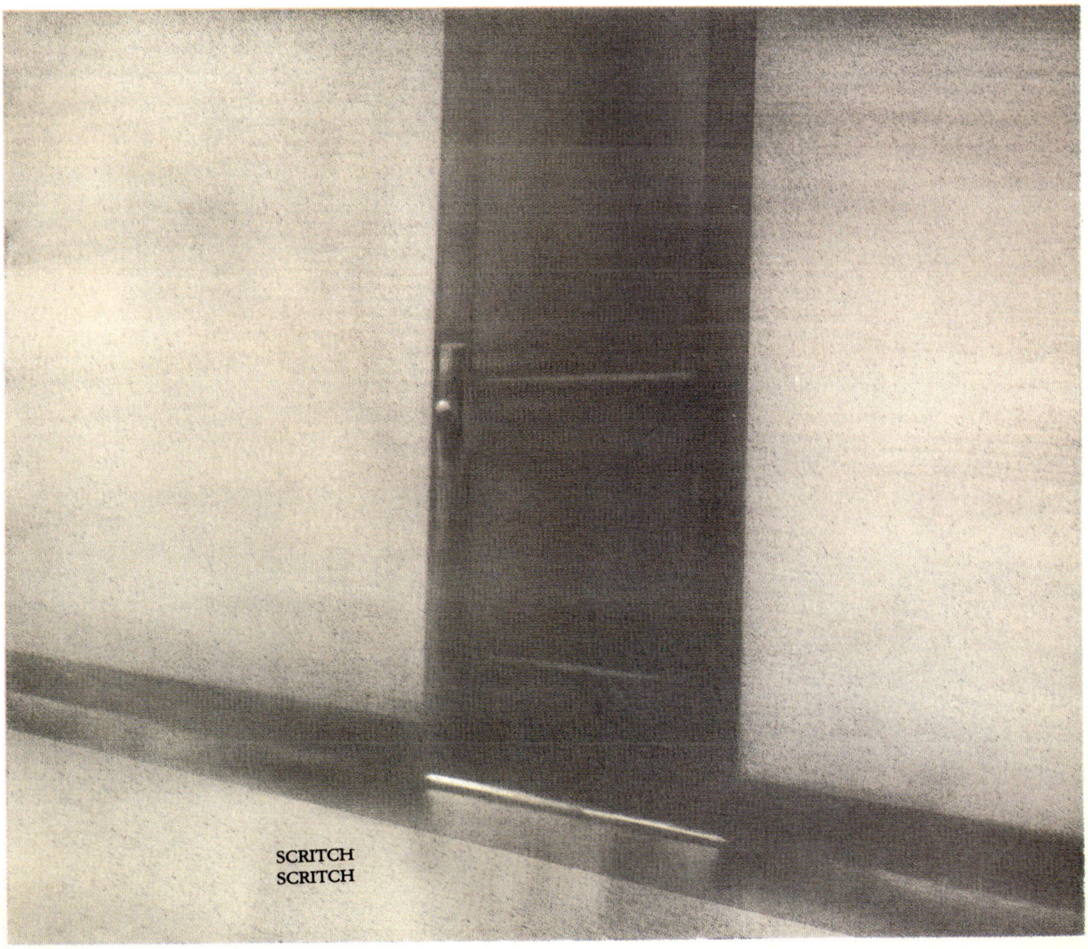
SCRITCH
SCRITCH

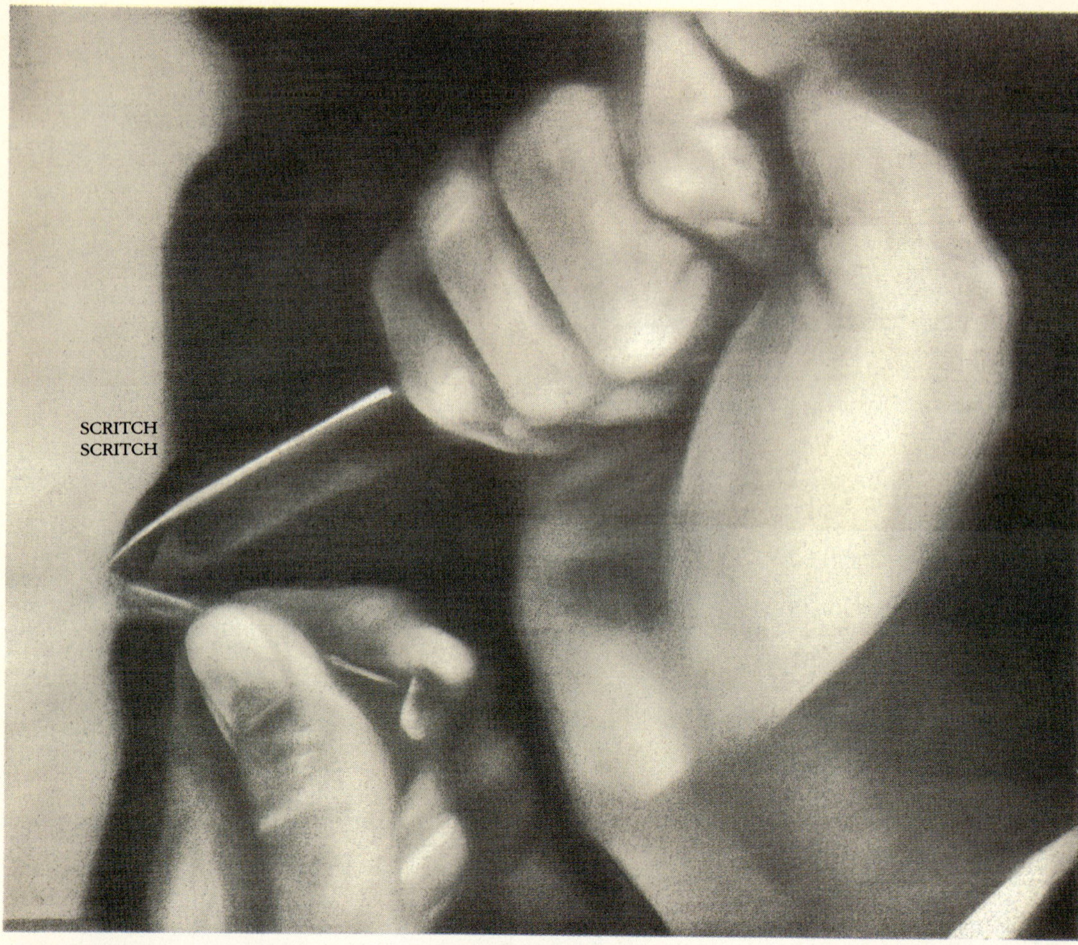
SCRITCH
SCRITCH

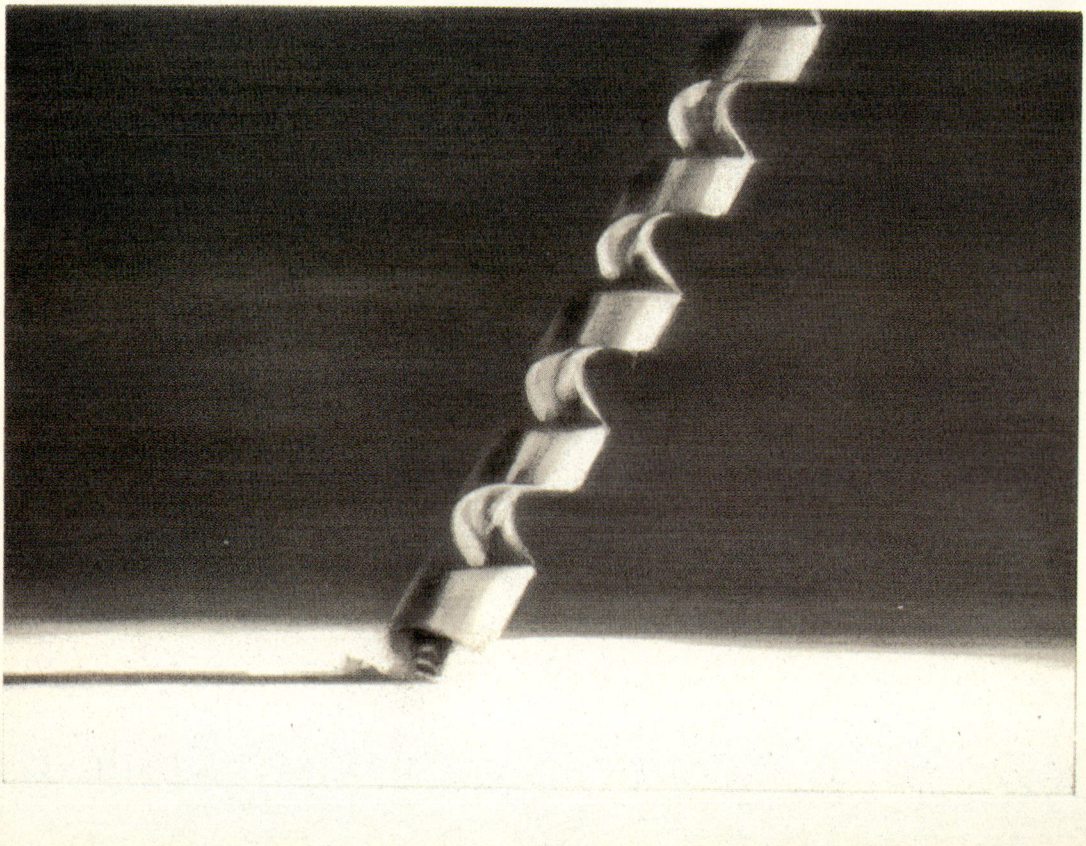

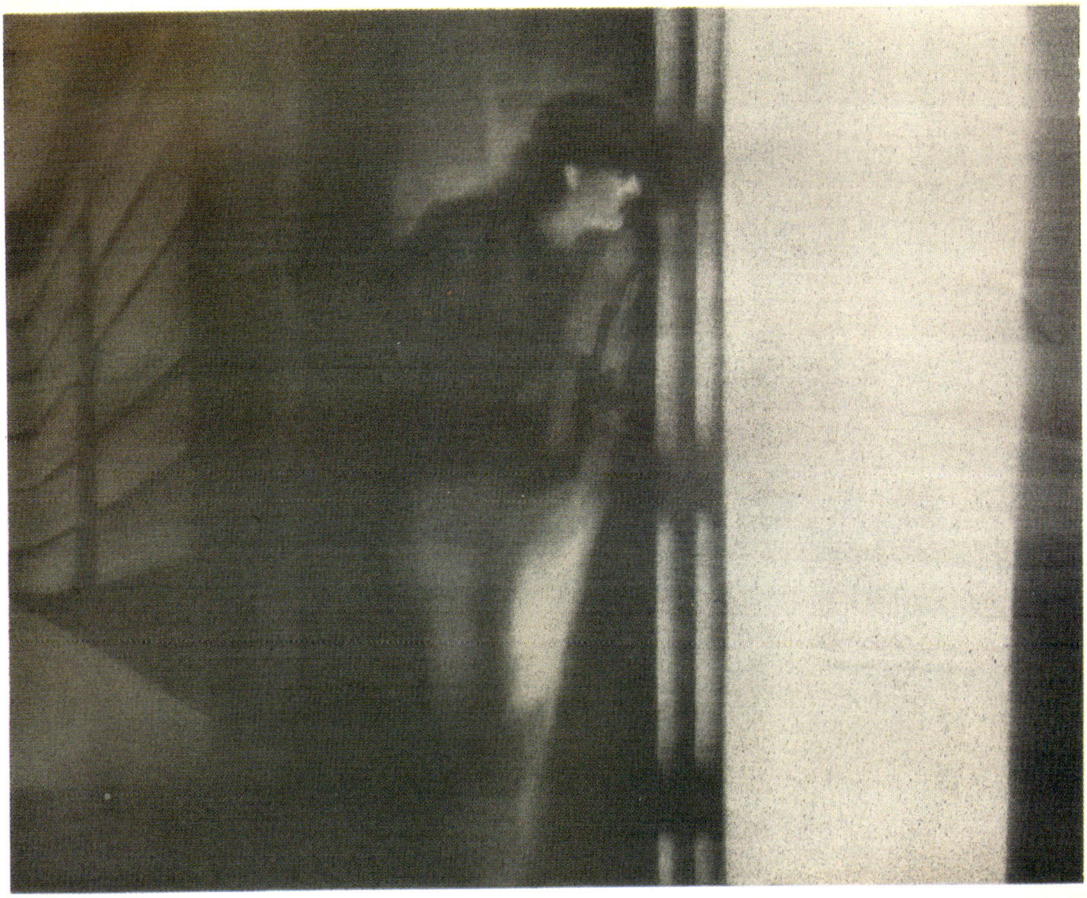

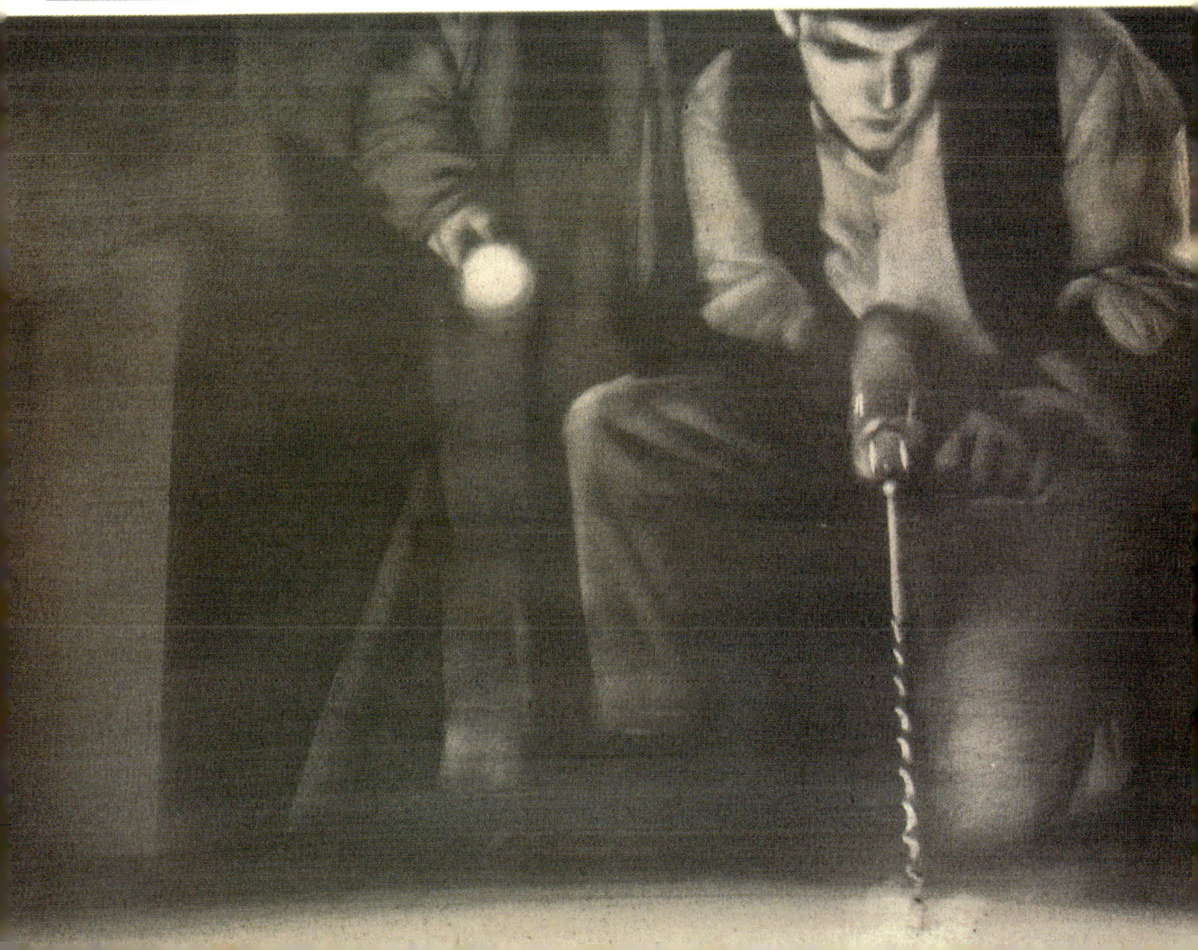

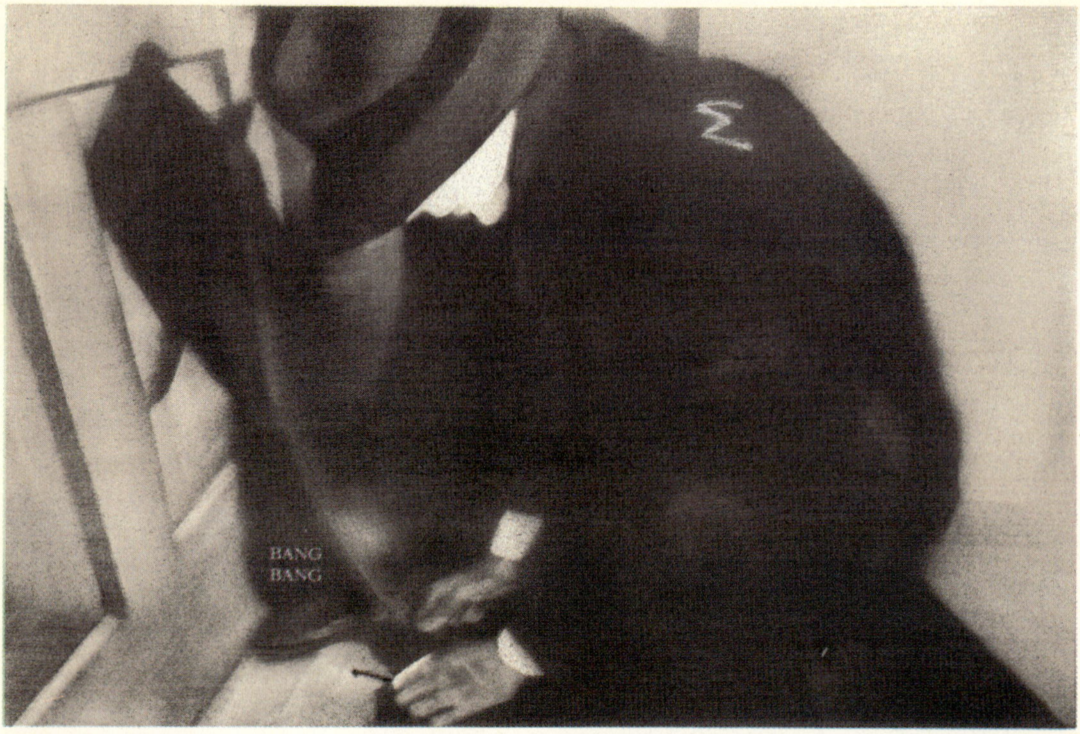
BANG
BANG

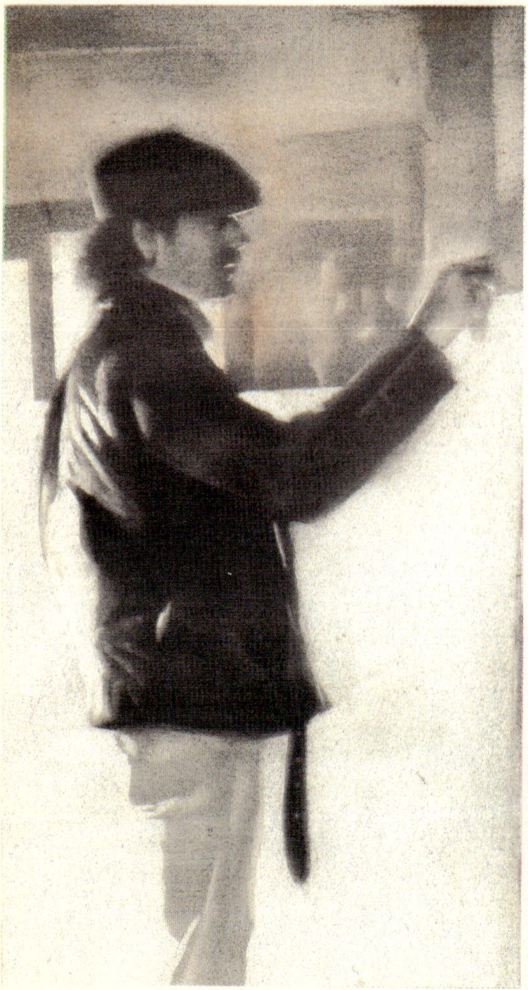

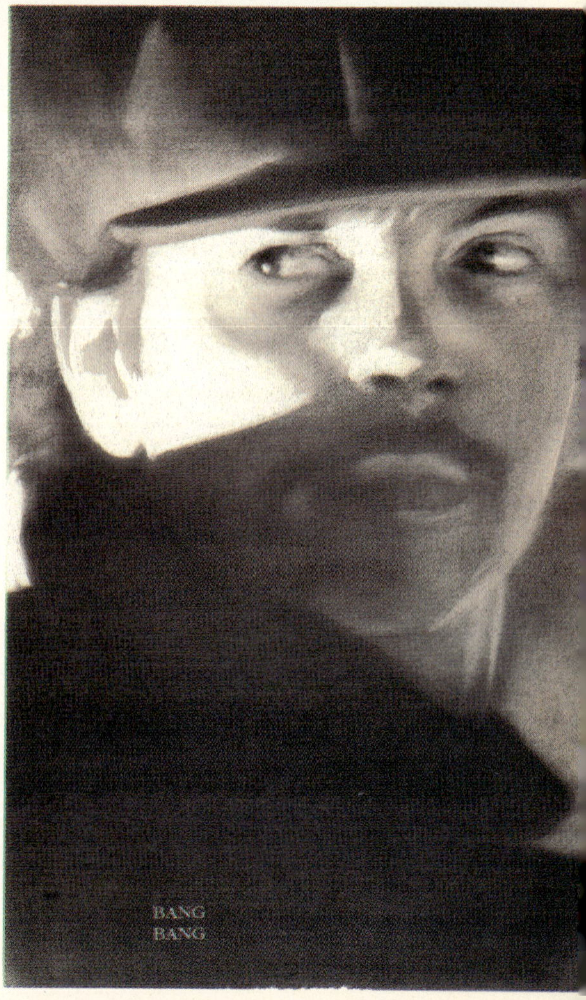
BANG
BANG

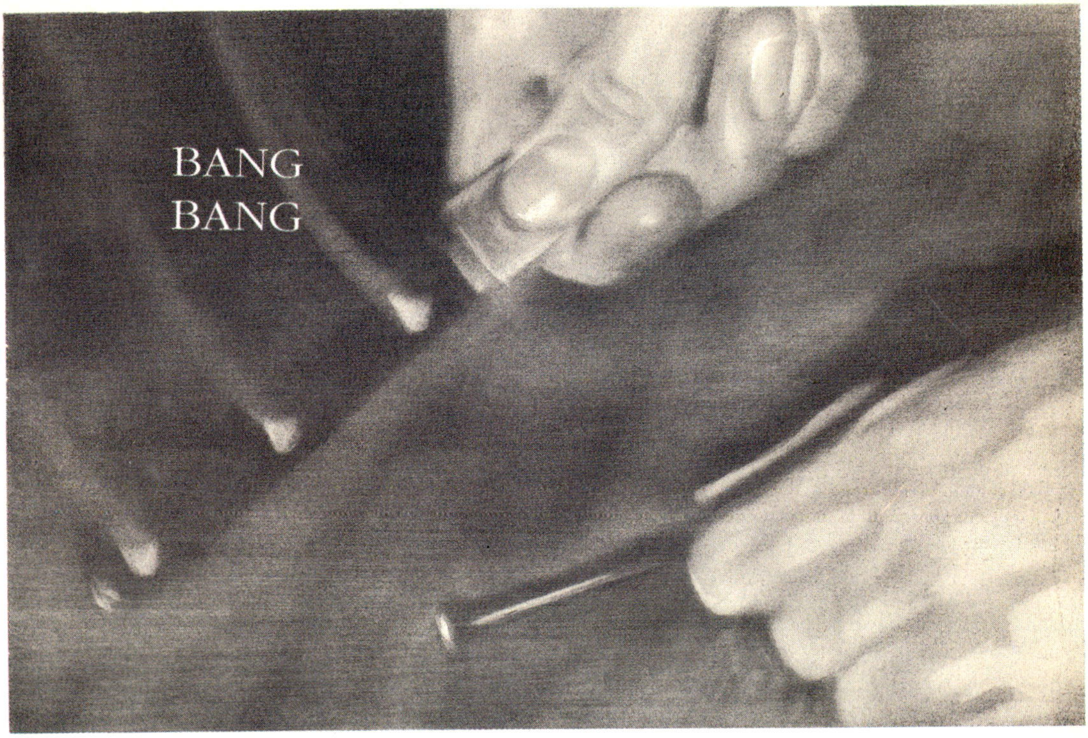
BANG
BANG

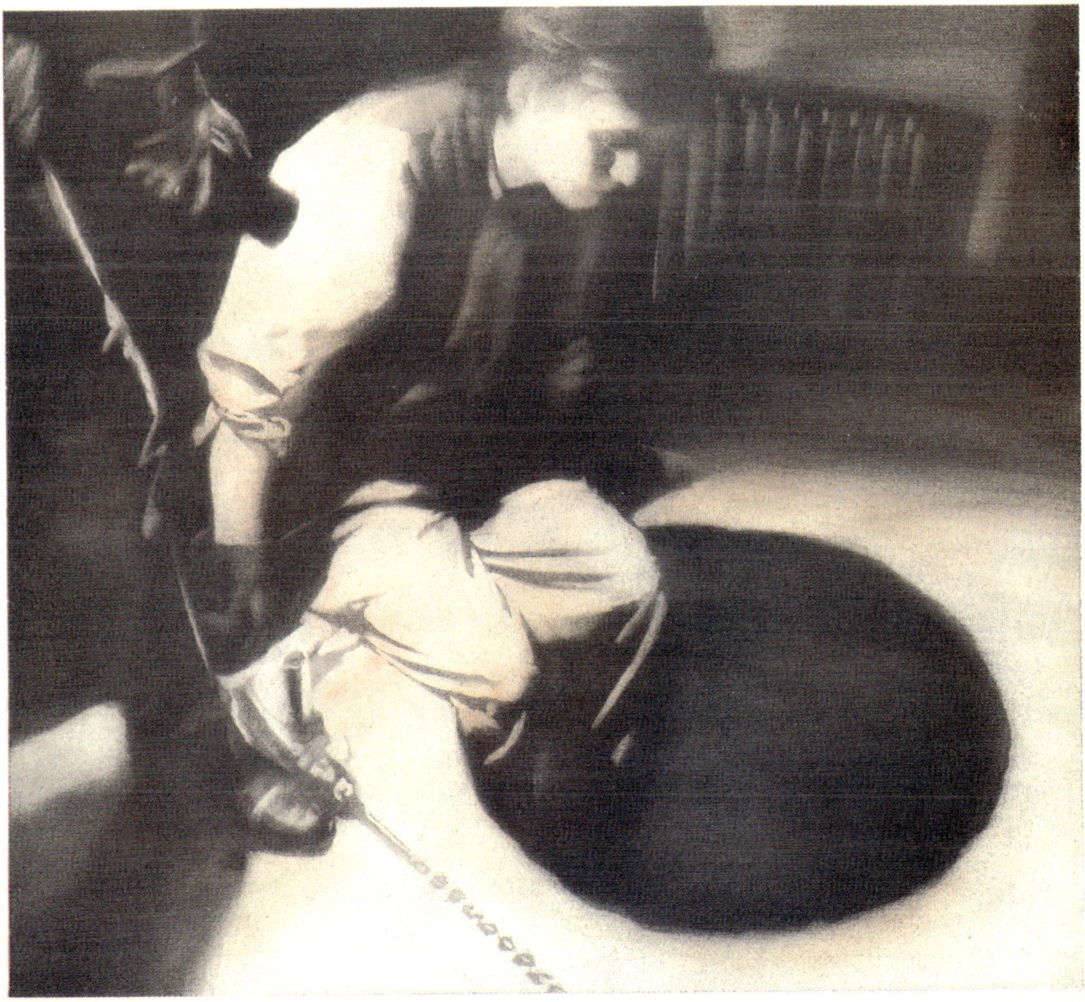

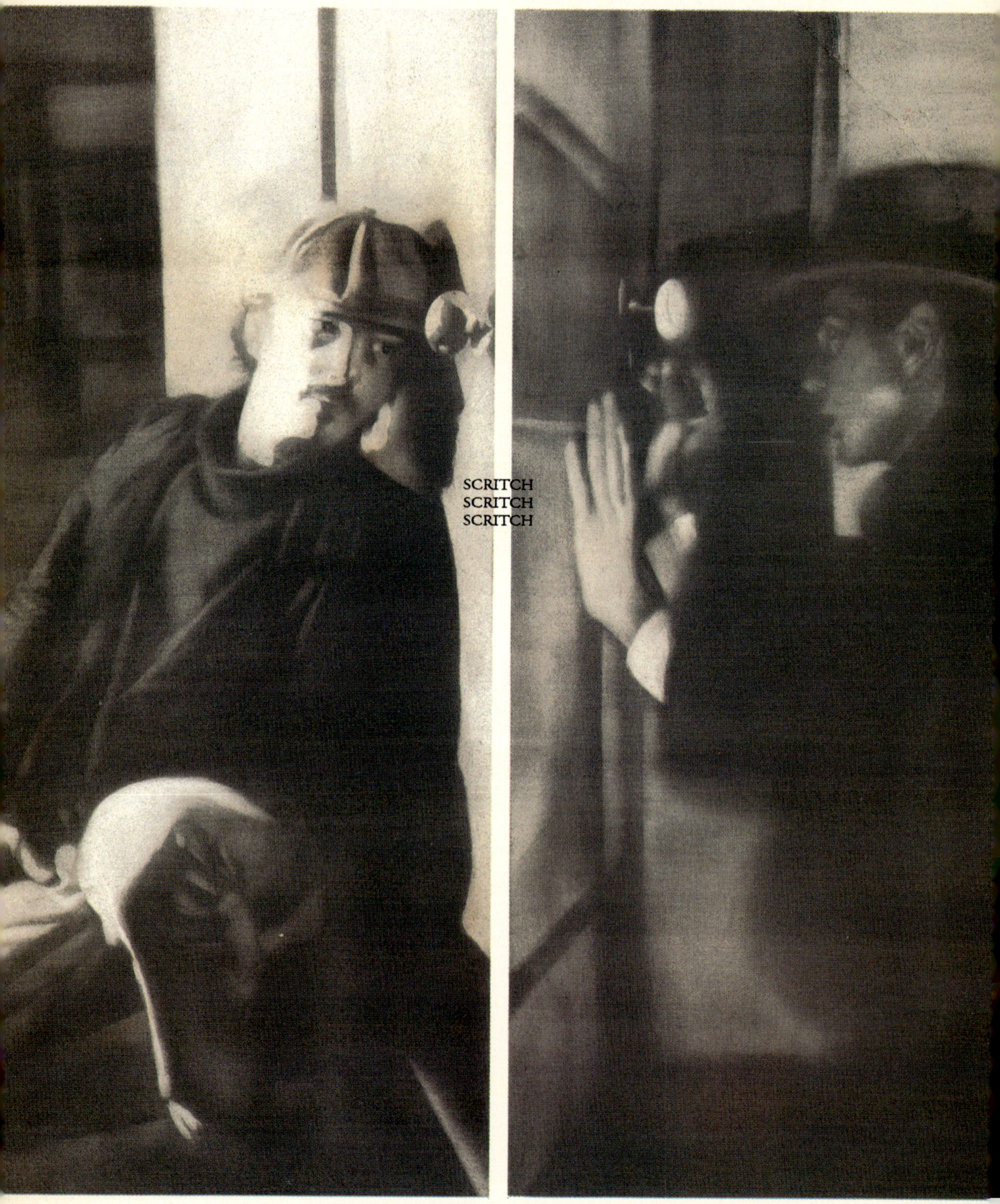
SCRITCH
SCRITCH
SCRITCH

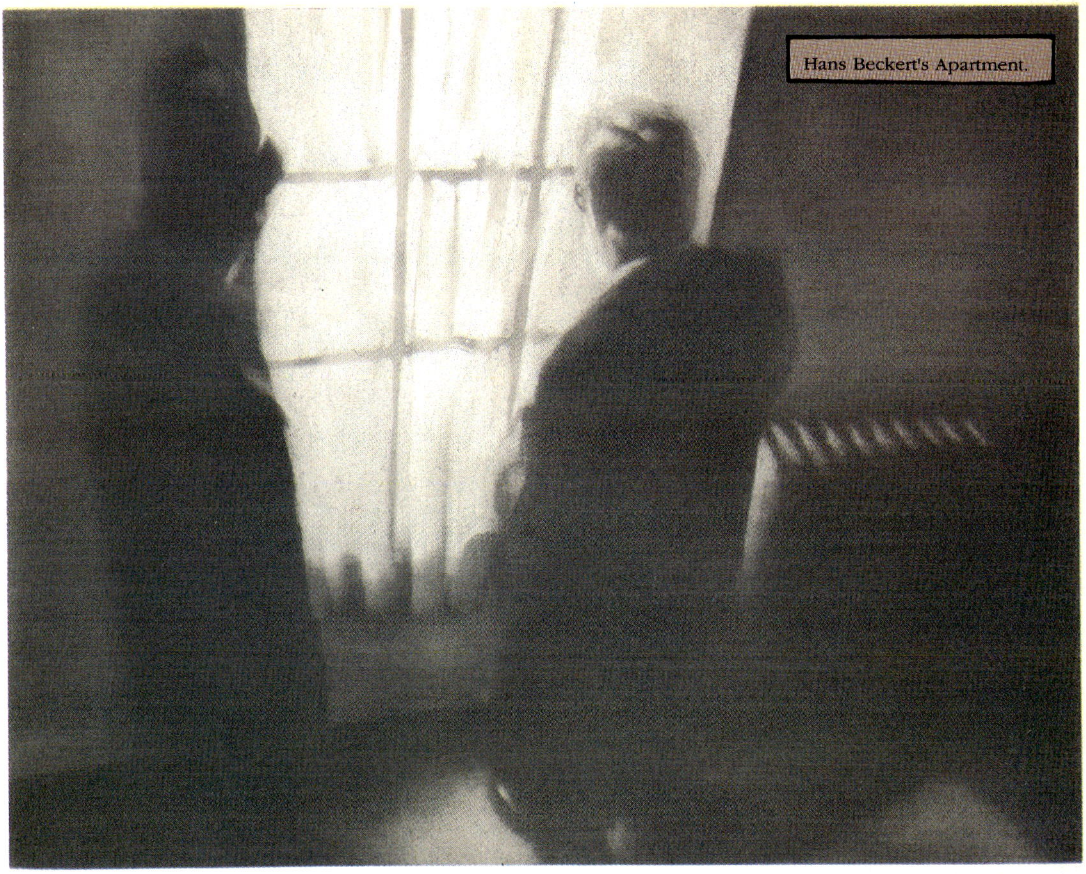
Hans Beckert's Apartment.

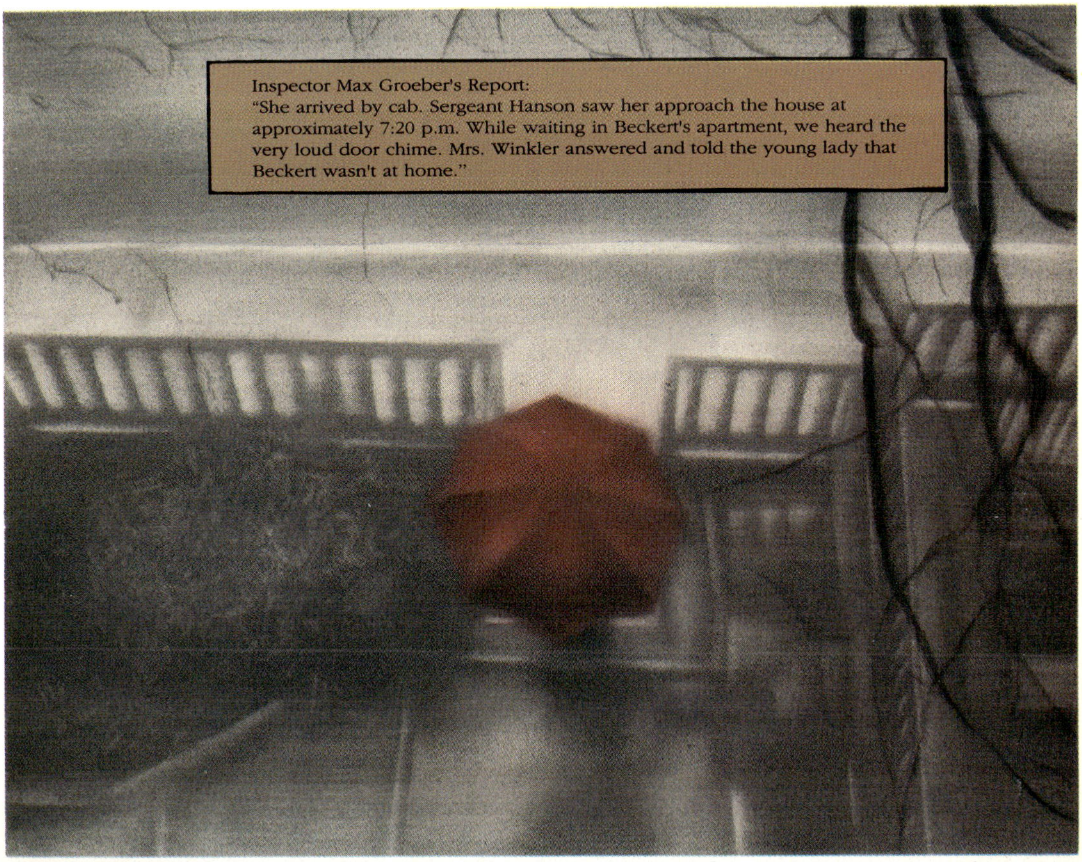
Inspector Max Groeber's Report:
"She arrived by cab. Sergeant Hanson saw her approach the house at approximately 7:20 p.m. While waiting in Beckert's apartment, we heard the very loud door chime. Mrs. Winkler answered and told the young lady that Beckert wasn't at home."

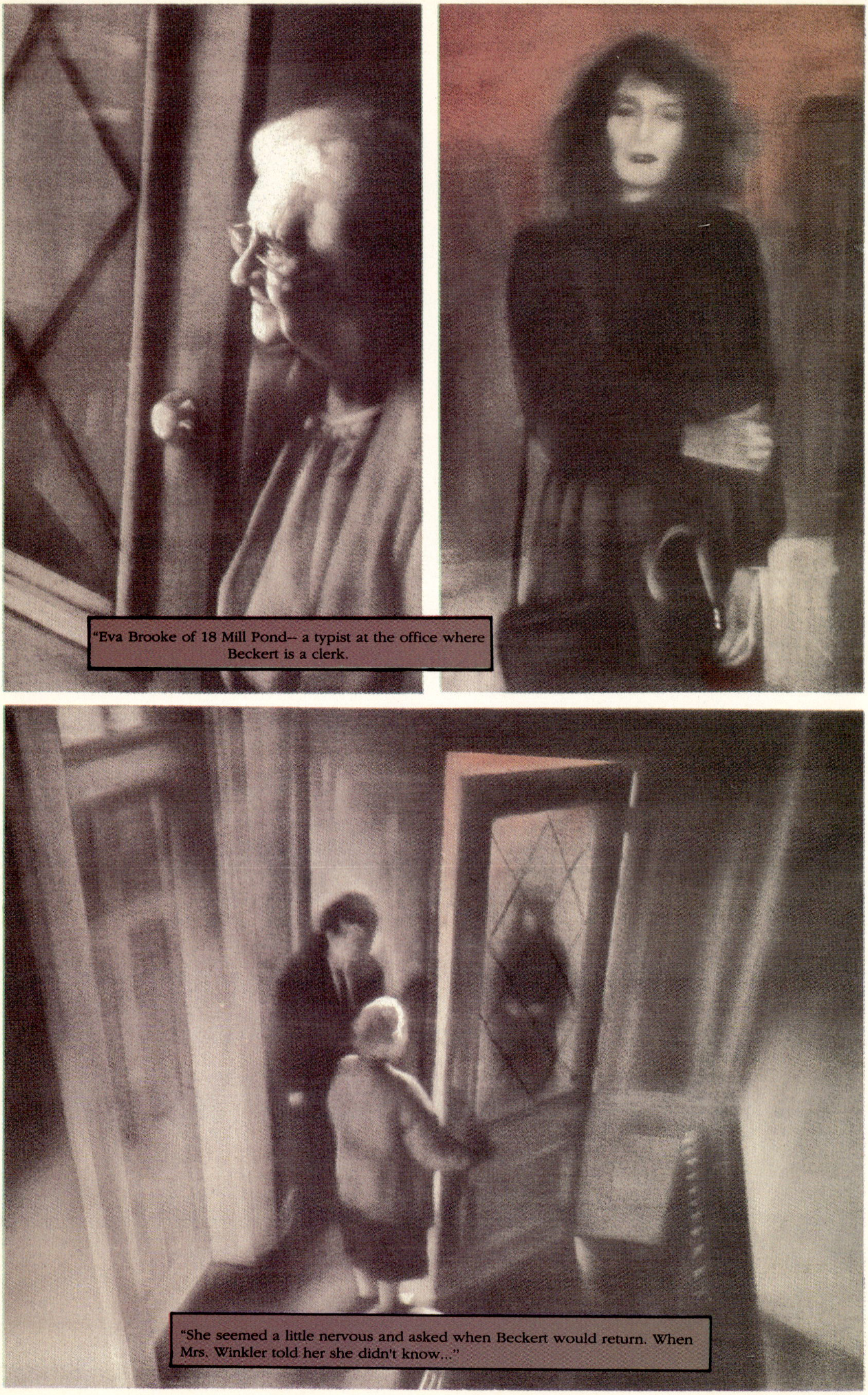
"Eva Brooke of 18 Mill Pond-- a typist at the office where Beckert is a clerk.
"She seemed a little nervous and asked when Beckert would return. When Mrs. Winkler told her she didn't know..."

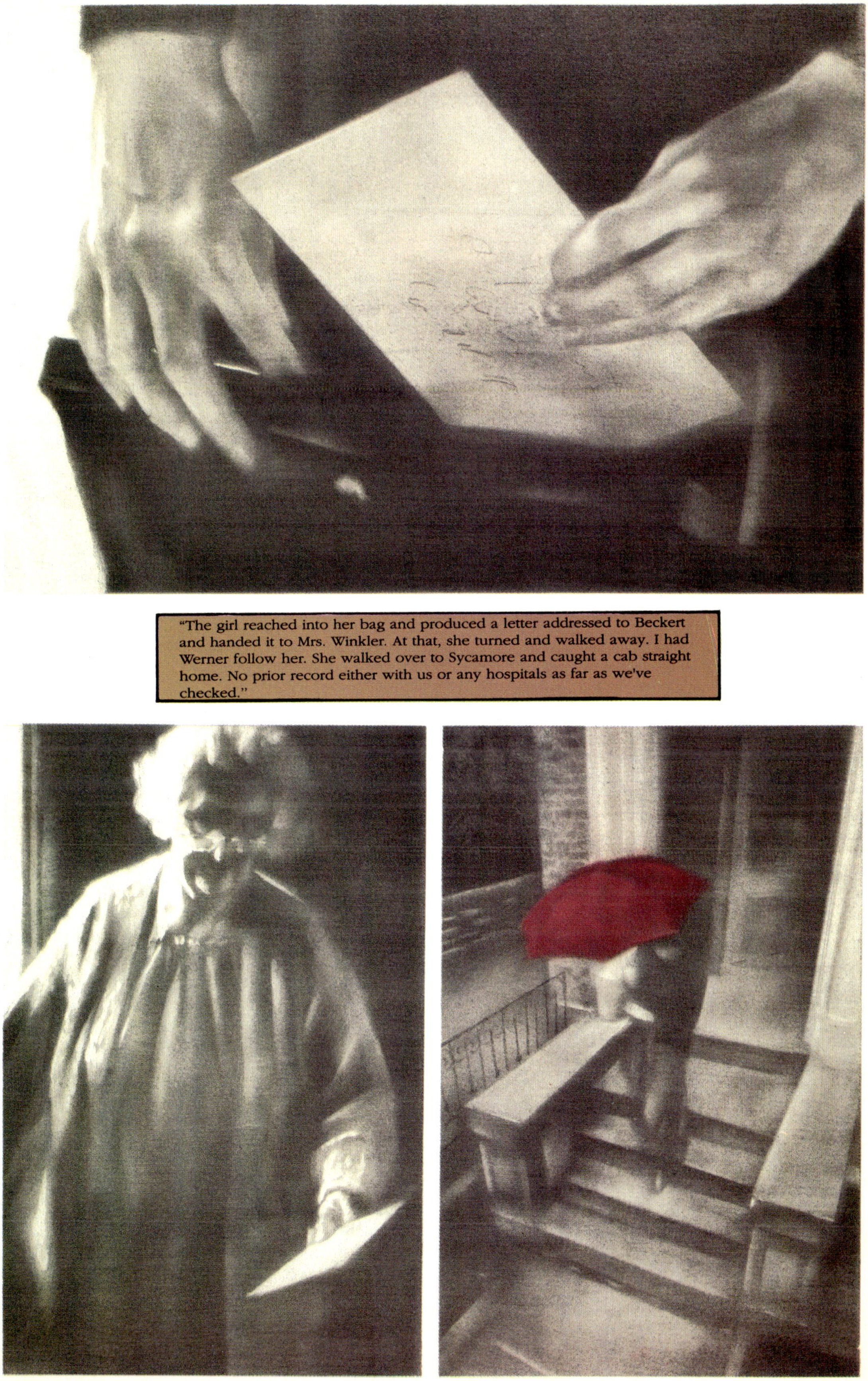
"The girl reached into her bag and produced a letter addressed to Beckert and handed it to Mrs. Winkler. At that, she turned and walked away. I had Werner follow her. She walked over to Sycamore and caught a cab straight home. No prior record either with us or any hospitals as far as we've checked."

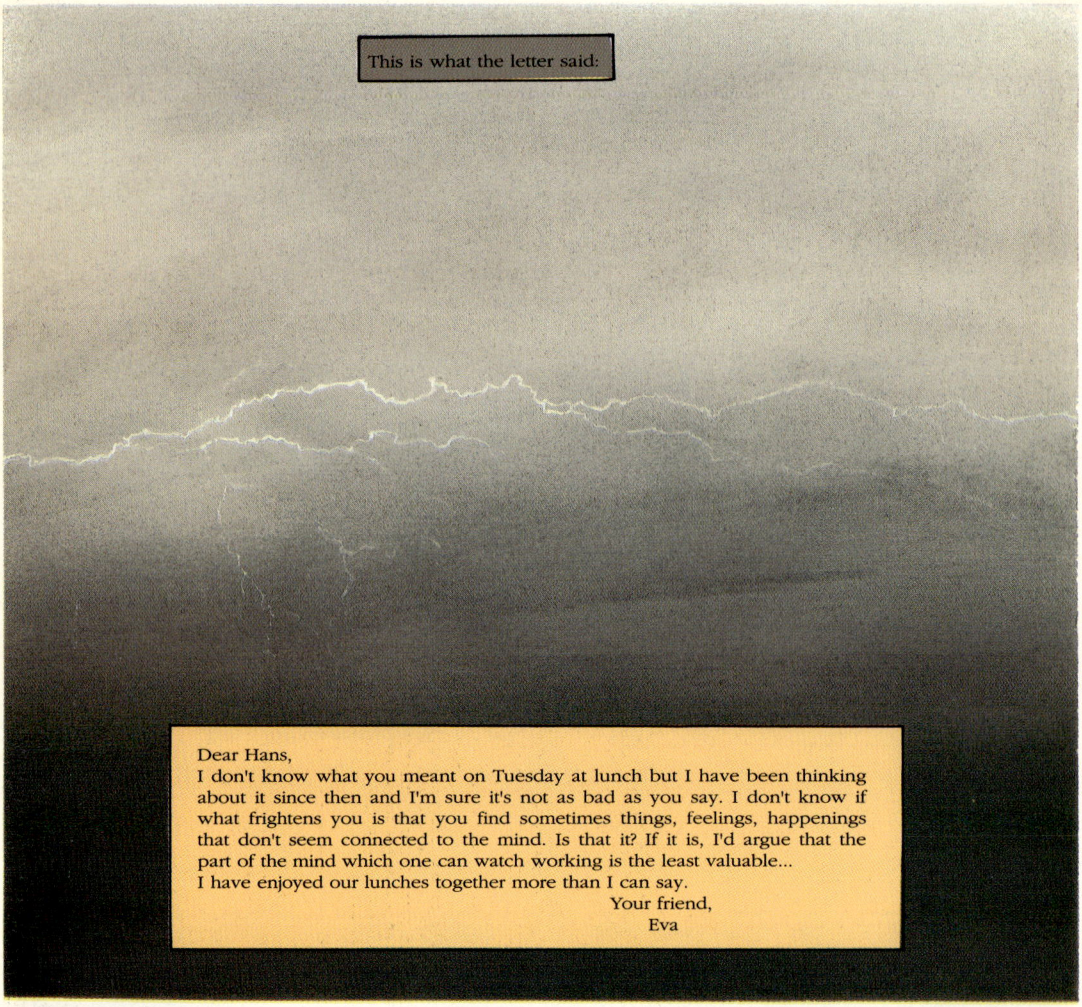
This is what the letter said:
Dear Hans,
I don't know what you meant on Tuesday at lunch but I have been thinking about it since then and I'm sure it's not as bad as you say. I don't know if what frightens you is that you find sometimes things, feelings, happenings that don't seem connected to the mind. Is that it? If it is, I'd argue that the part of the mind which one can watch working is the least valuable...
I have enjoyed our lunches together more than I can say.
Your friend,
Eva

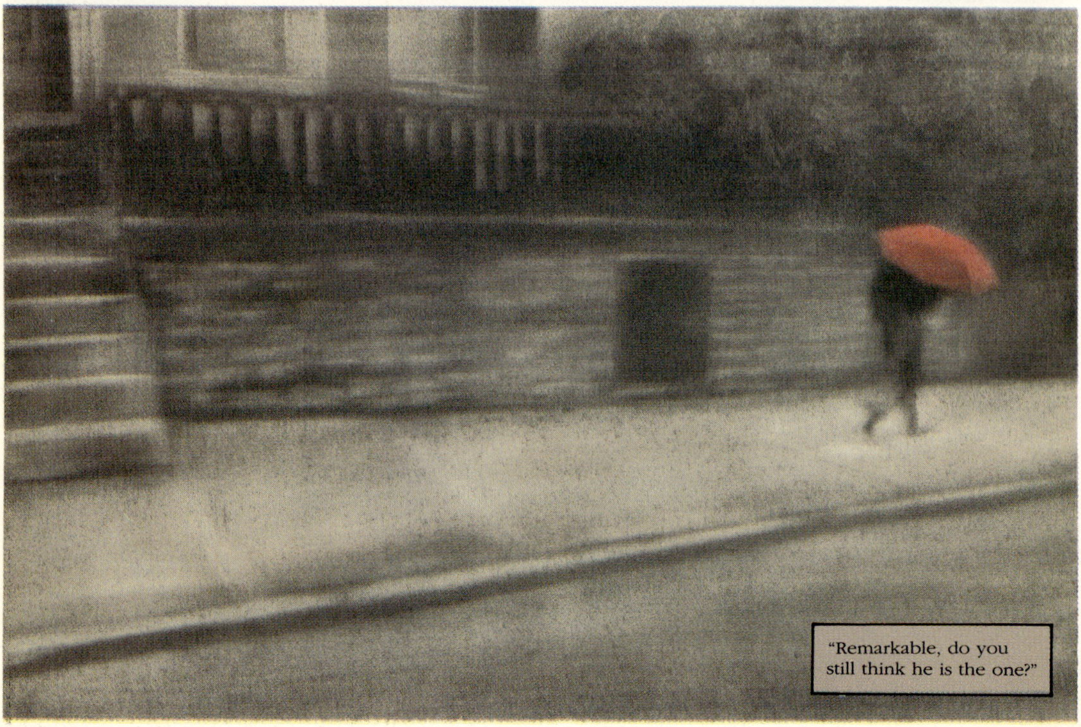
"Remarkable, do you still think he is the one?"

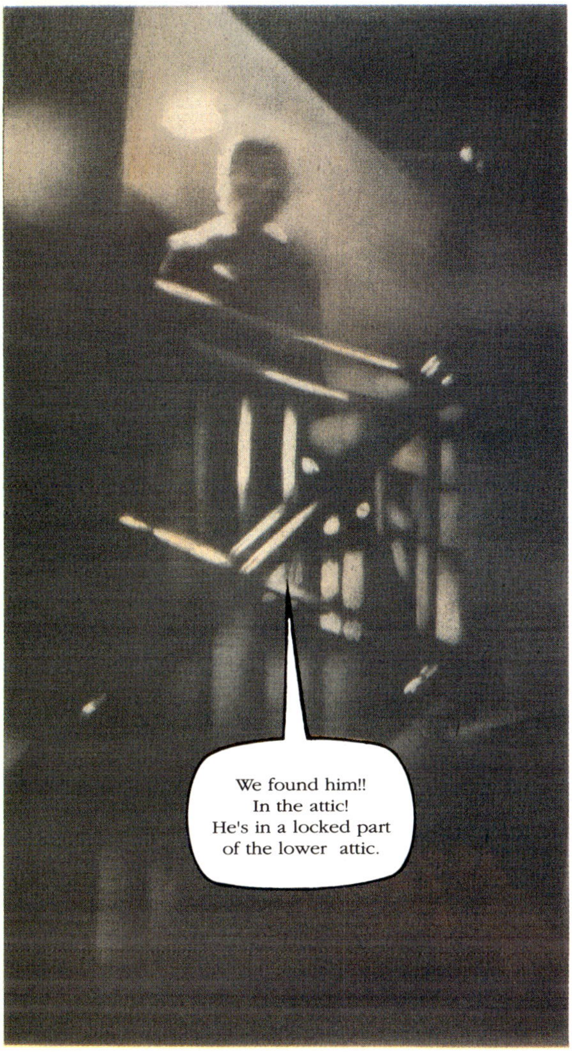
We found him!! In the attic! He's in a locked part of the lower attic.

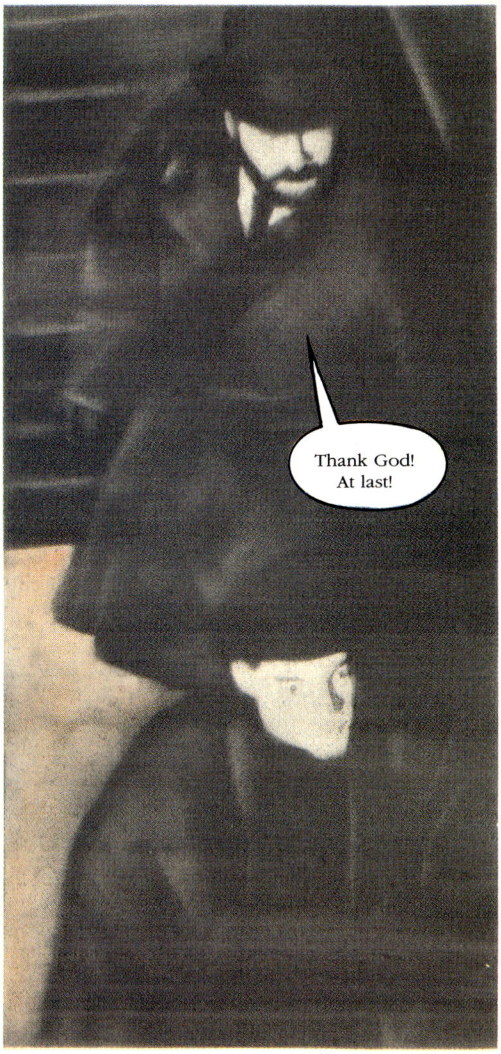
Thank God! At last!

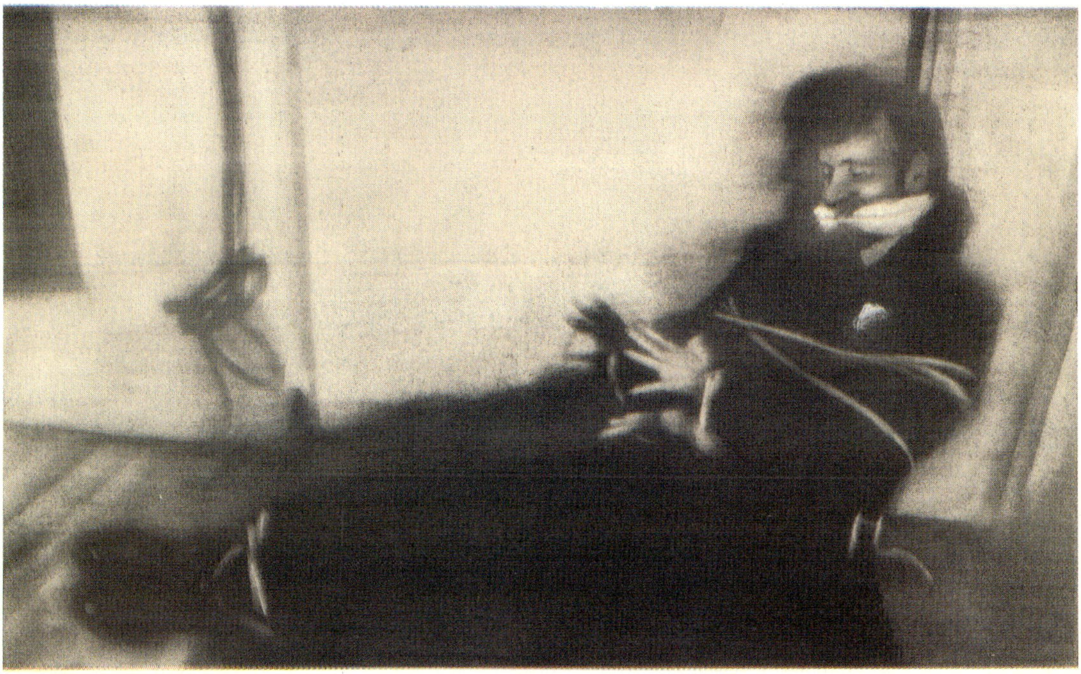

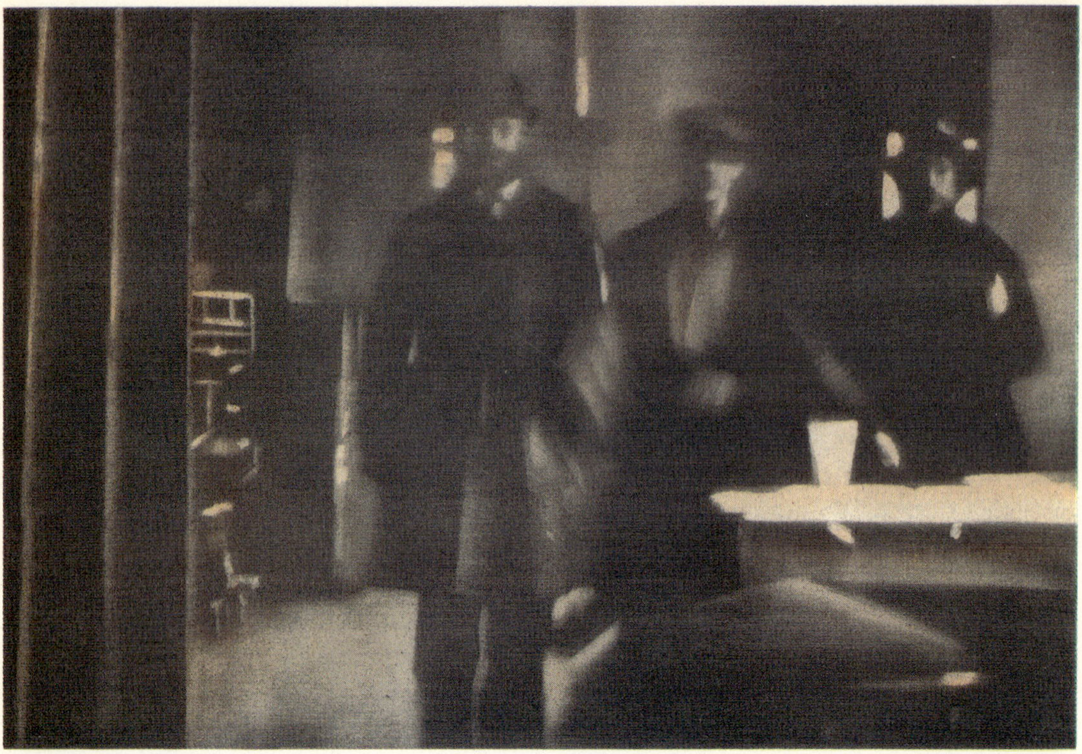

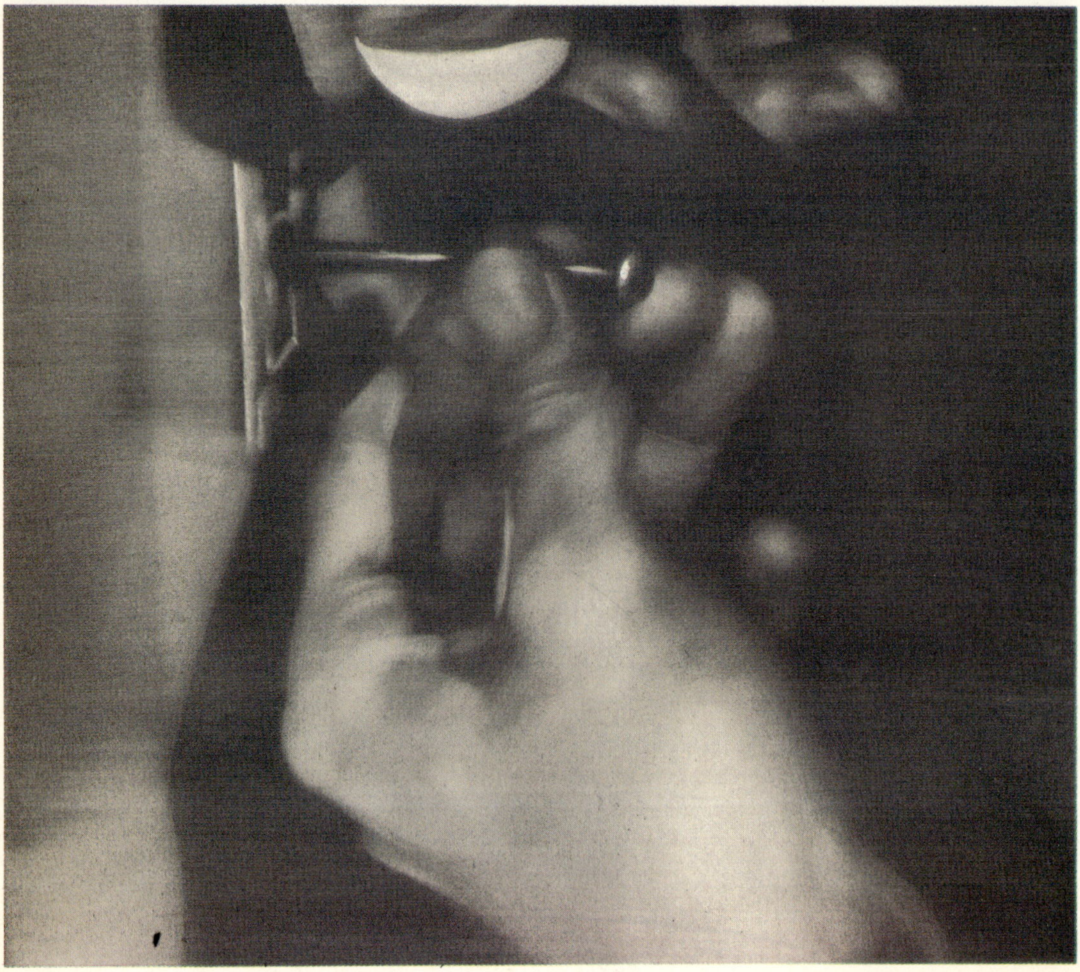

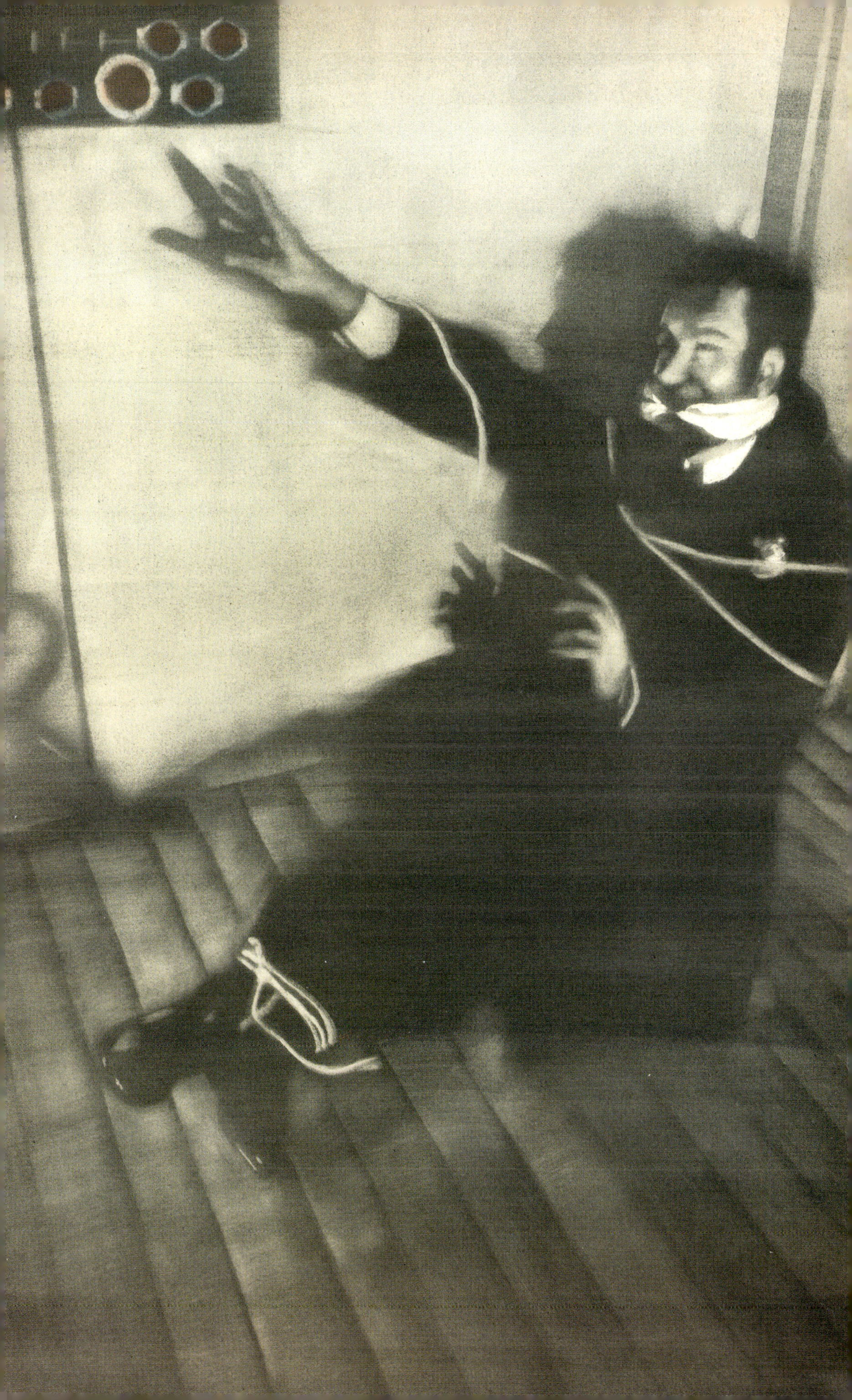

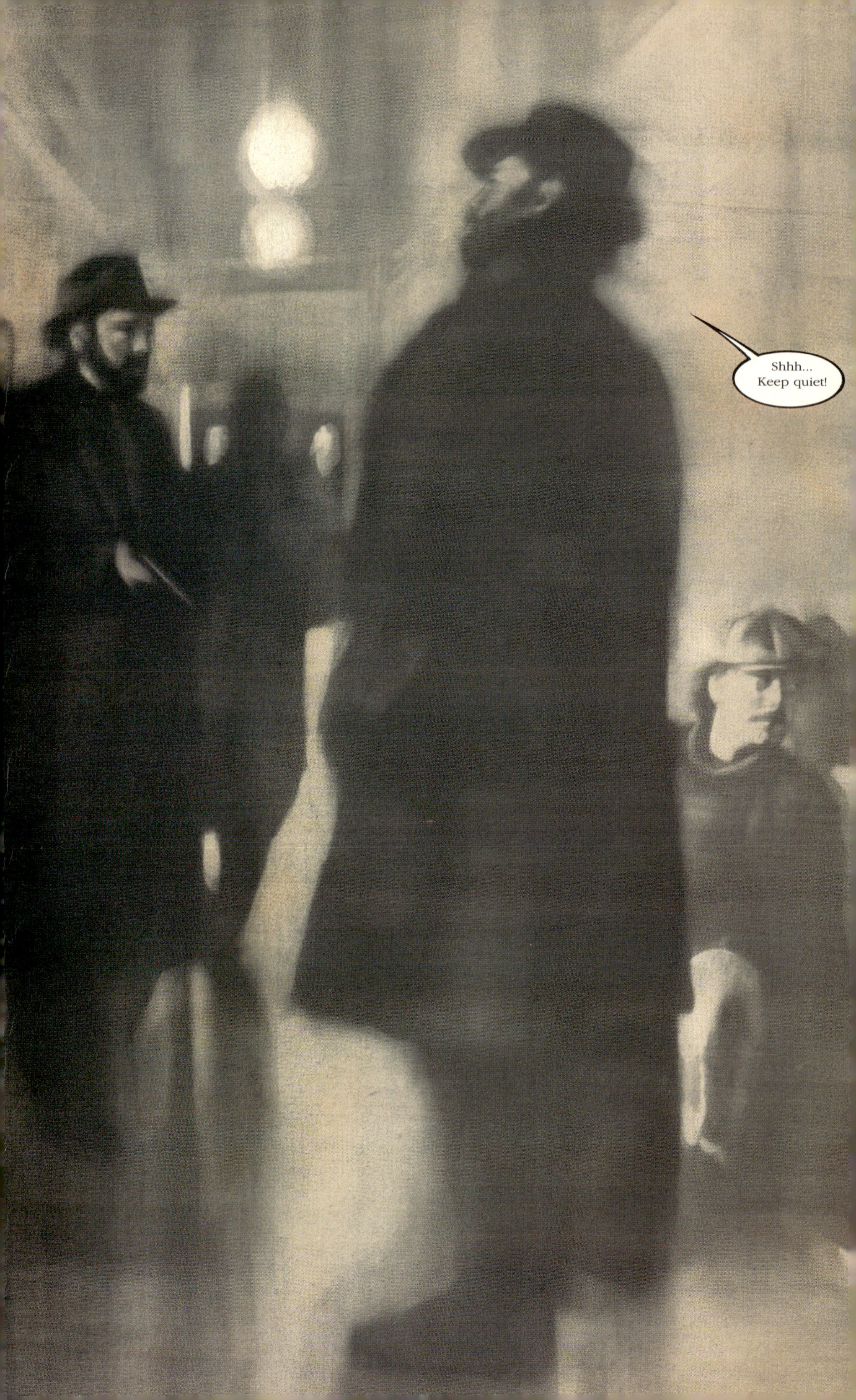
Shhh... Keep quiet!

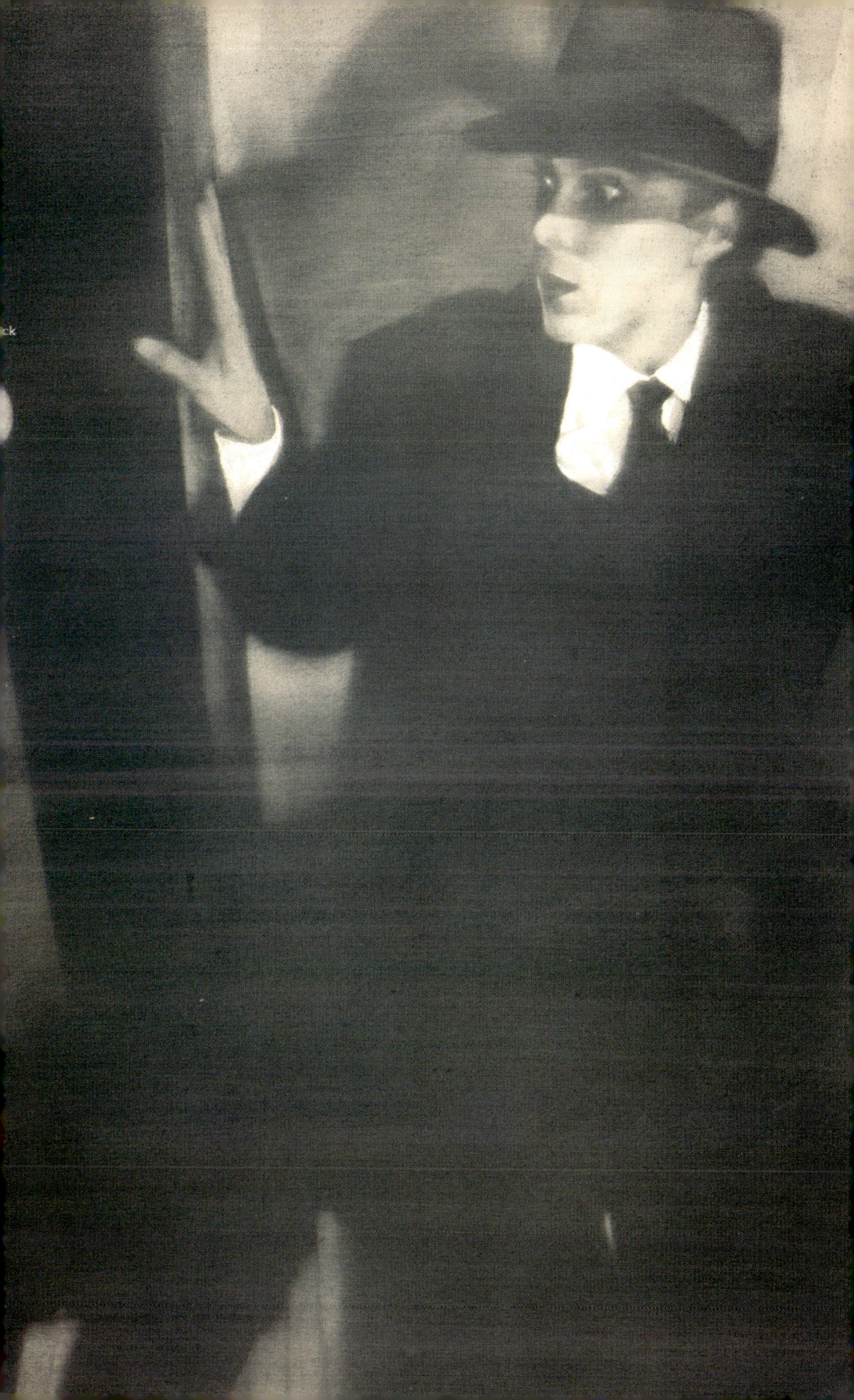

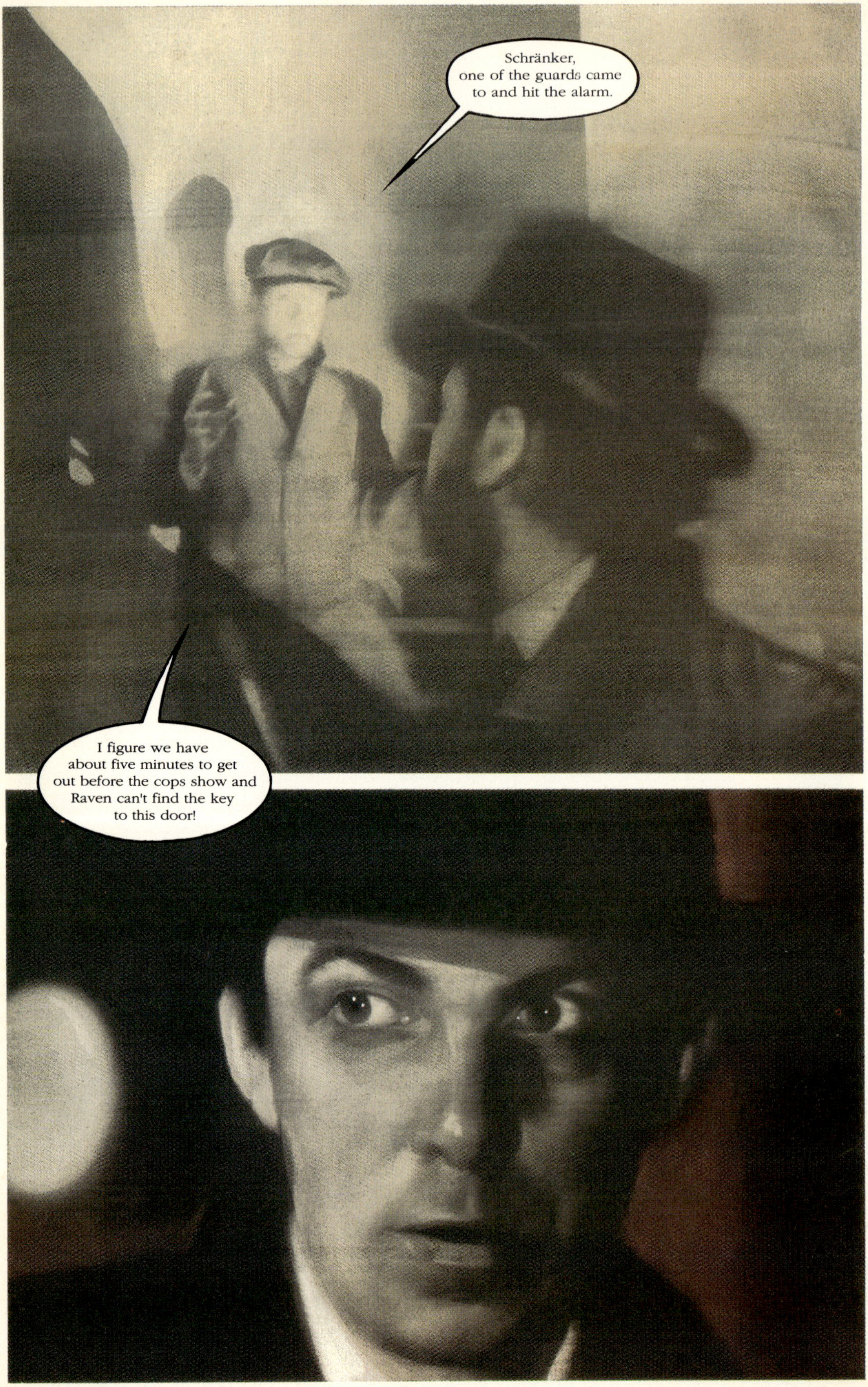
Schränker, one of the guards came to and hit the alarm.
I figure we have about five minutes to get out before the cops show and Raven can't find the key to this door!

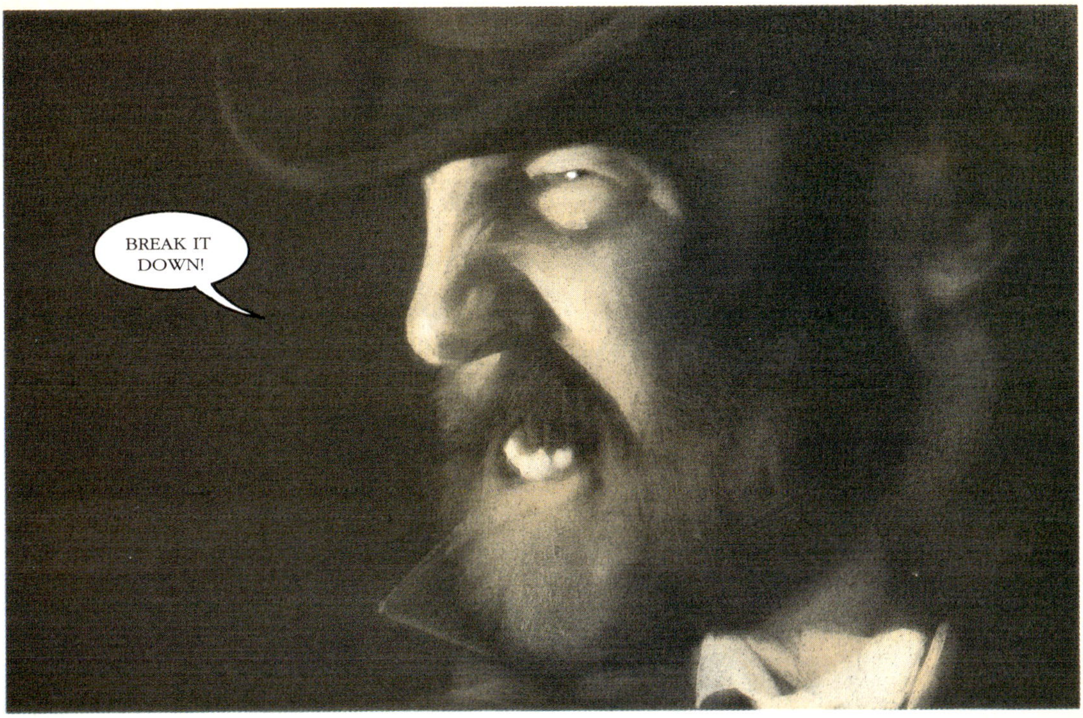
BREAK IT DOWN!

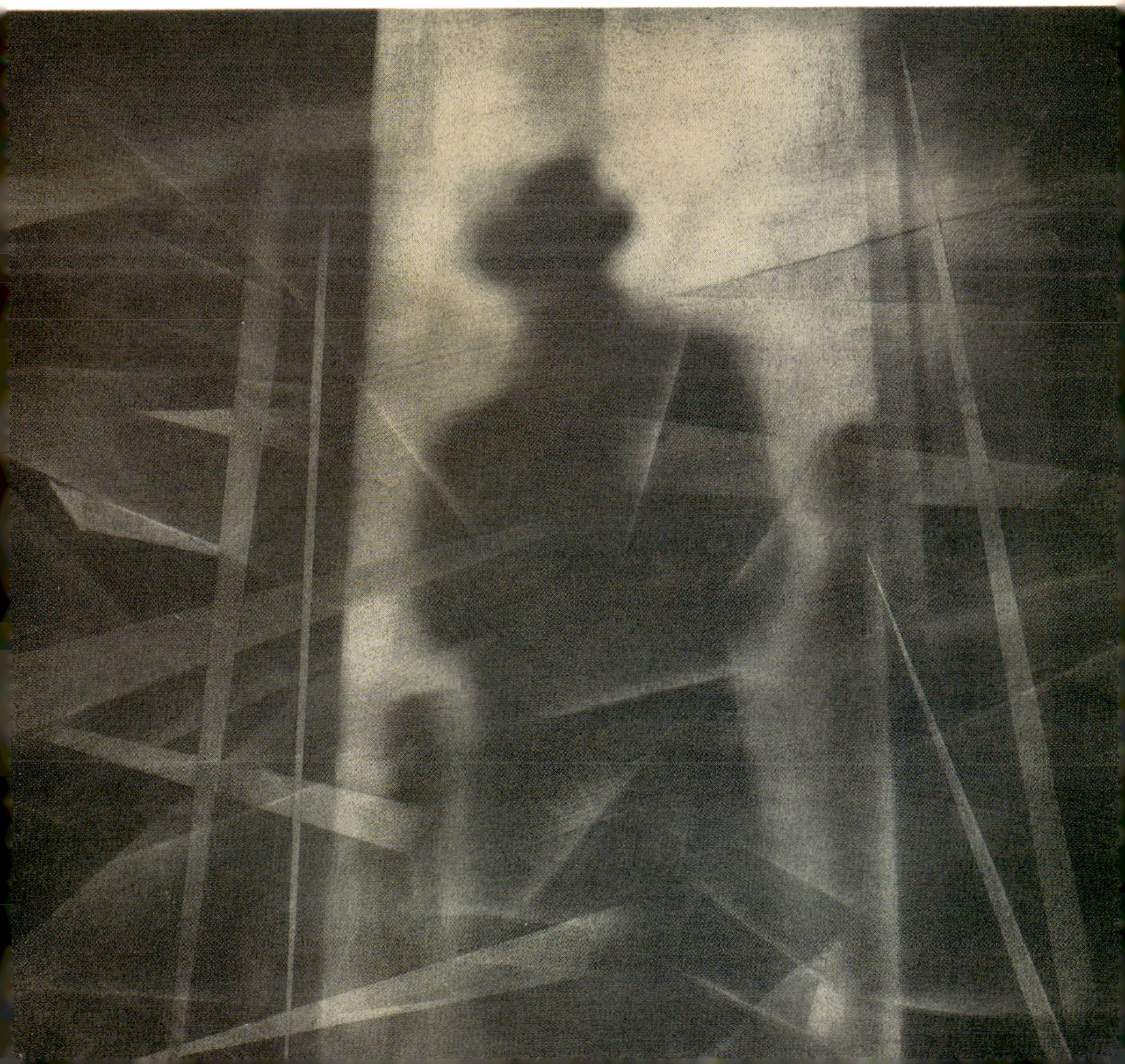

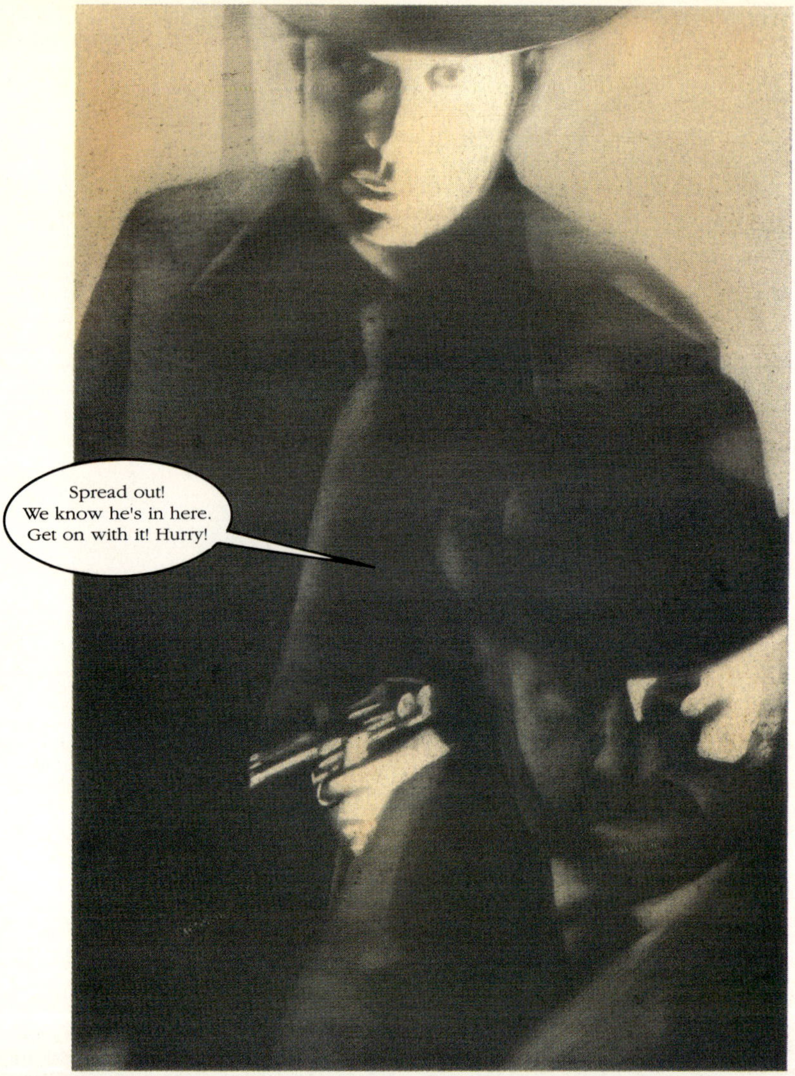
Spread out! We know he's in here. Get on with it! Hurry!

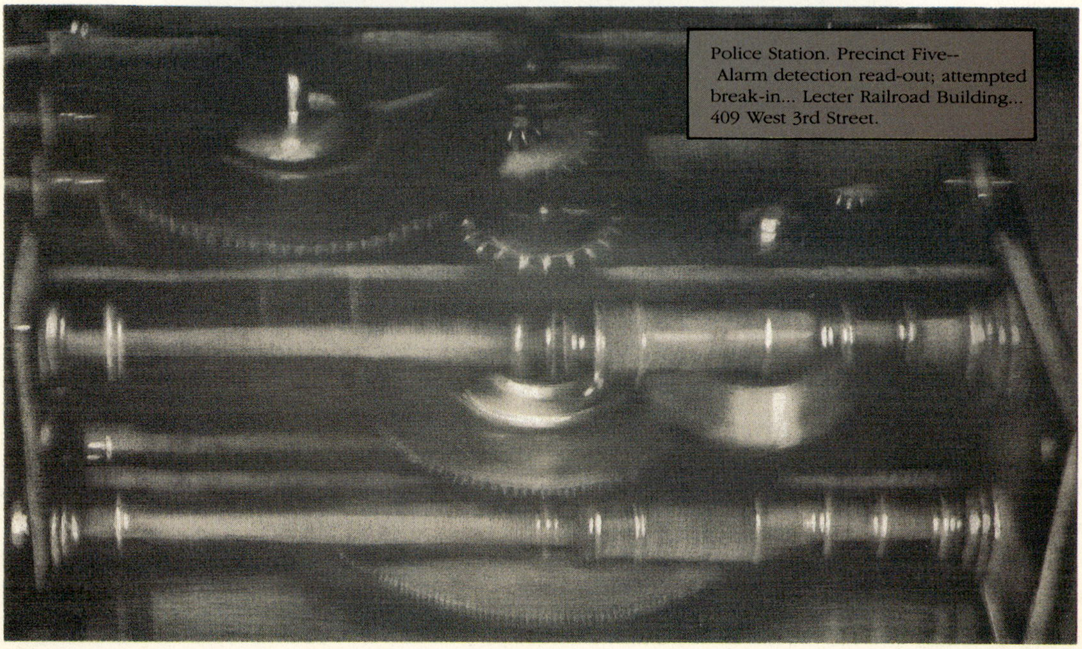
Police Station. Precinct Five-- Alarm detection read-out; attempted break-in... Lecter Railroad Building... 409 West 3rd Street.

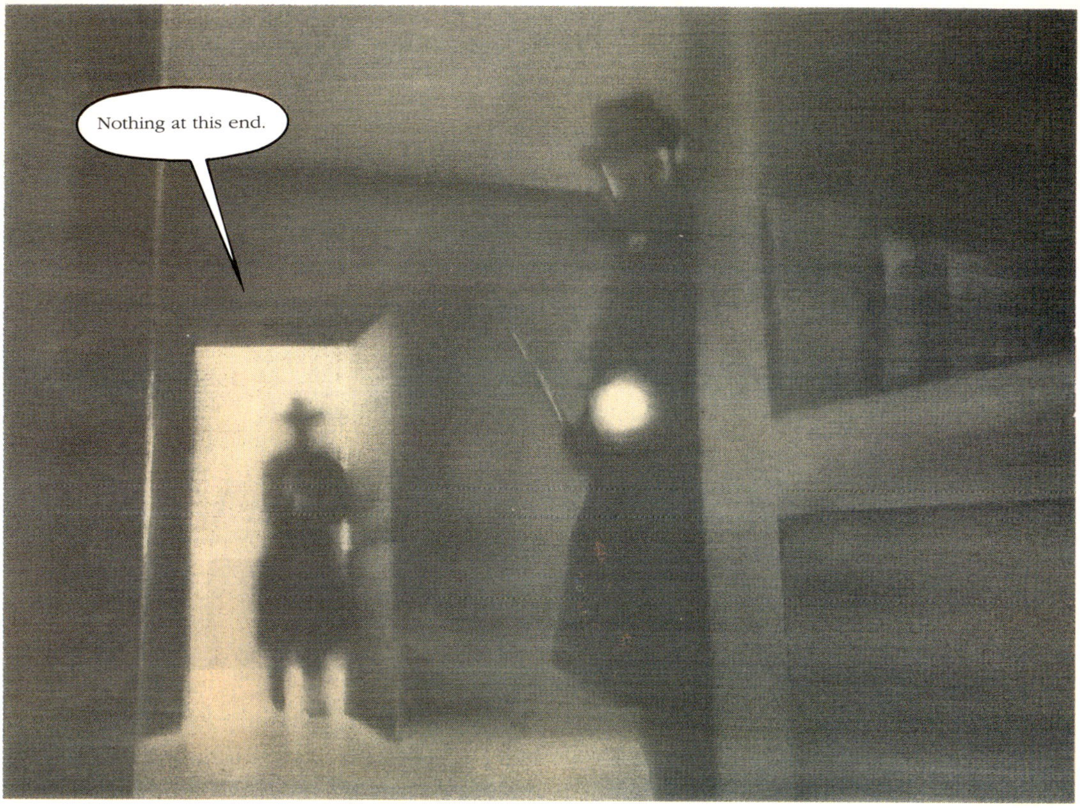
Nothing at this end.

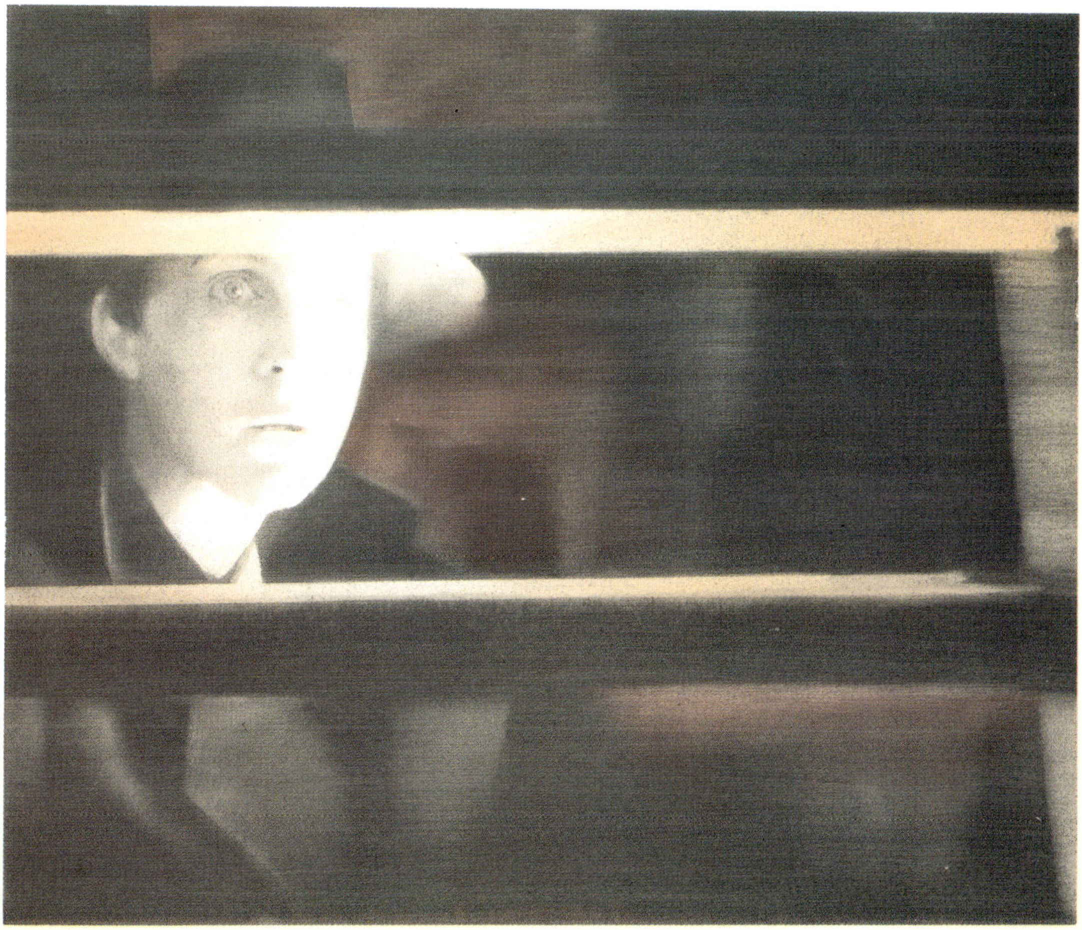

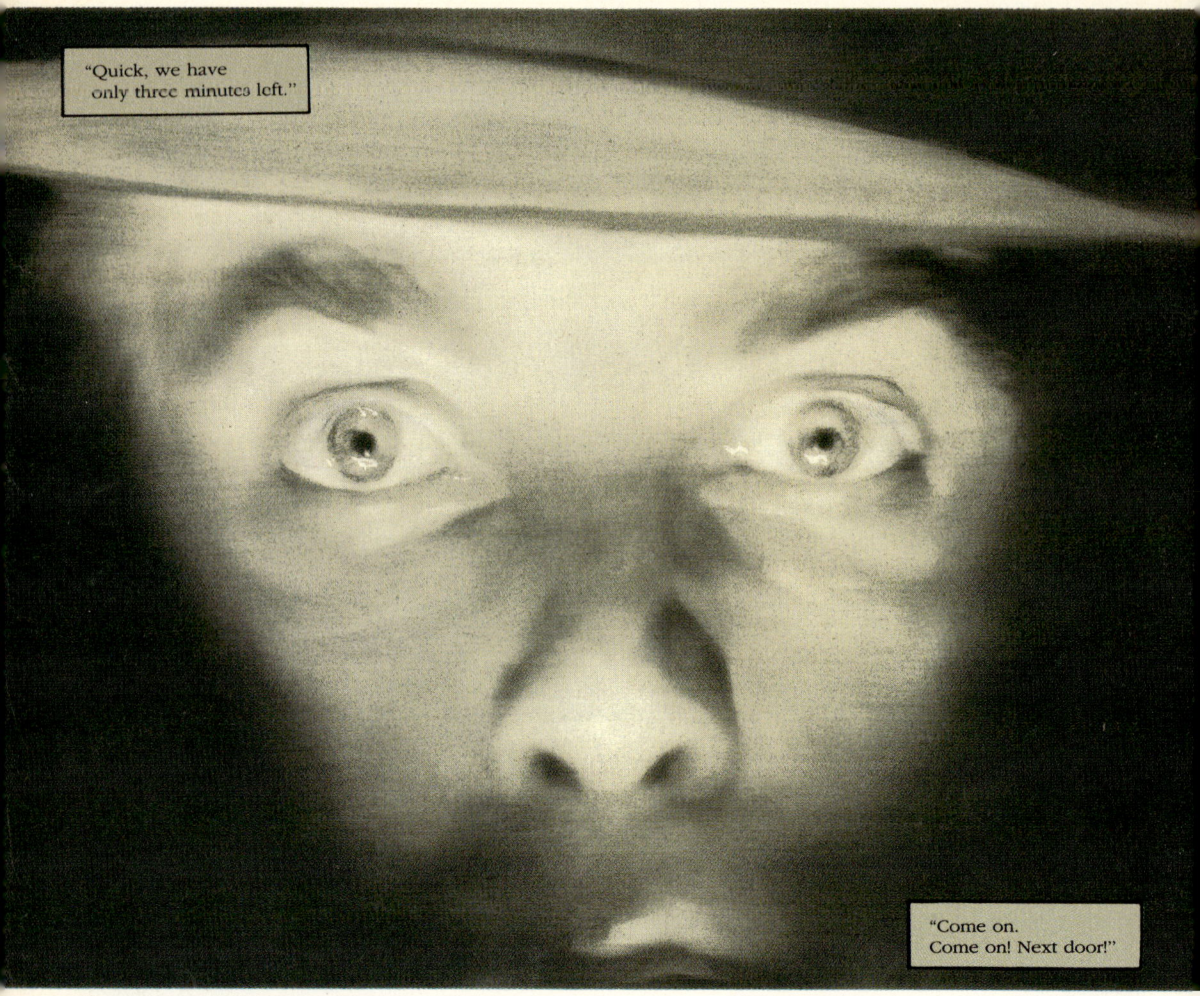
"Quick, we have only three minutes left."
"Come on. Come on! Next door!"

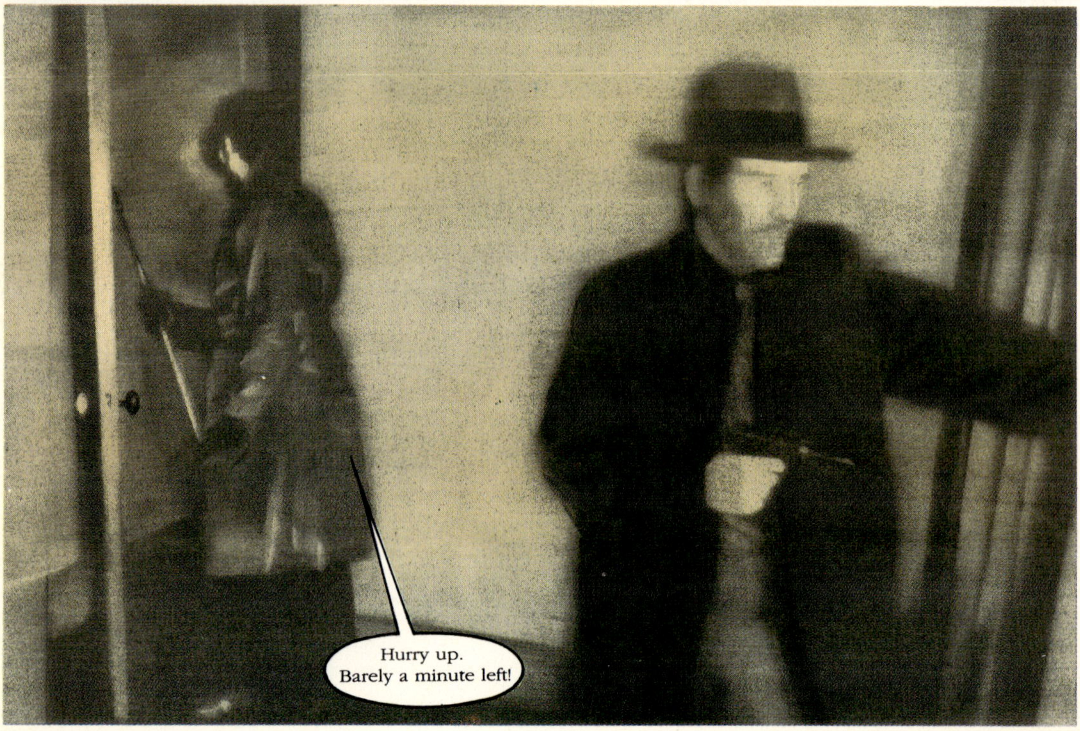
Hurry up. Barely a minute left!

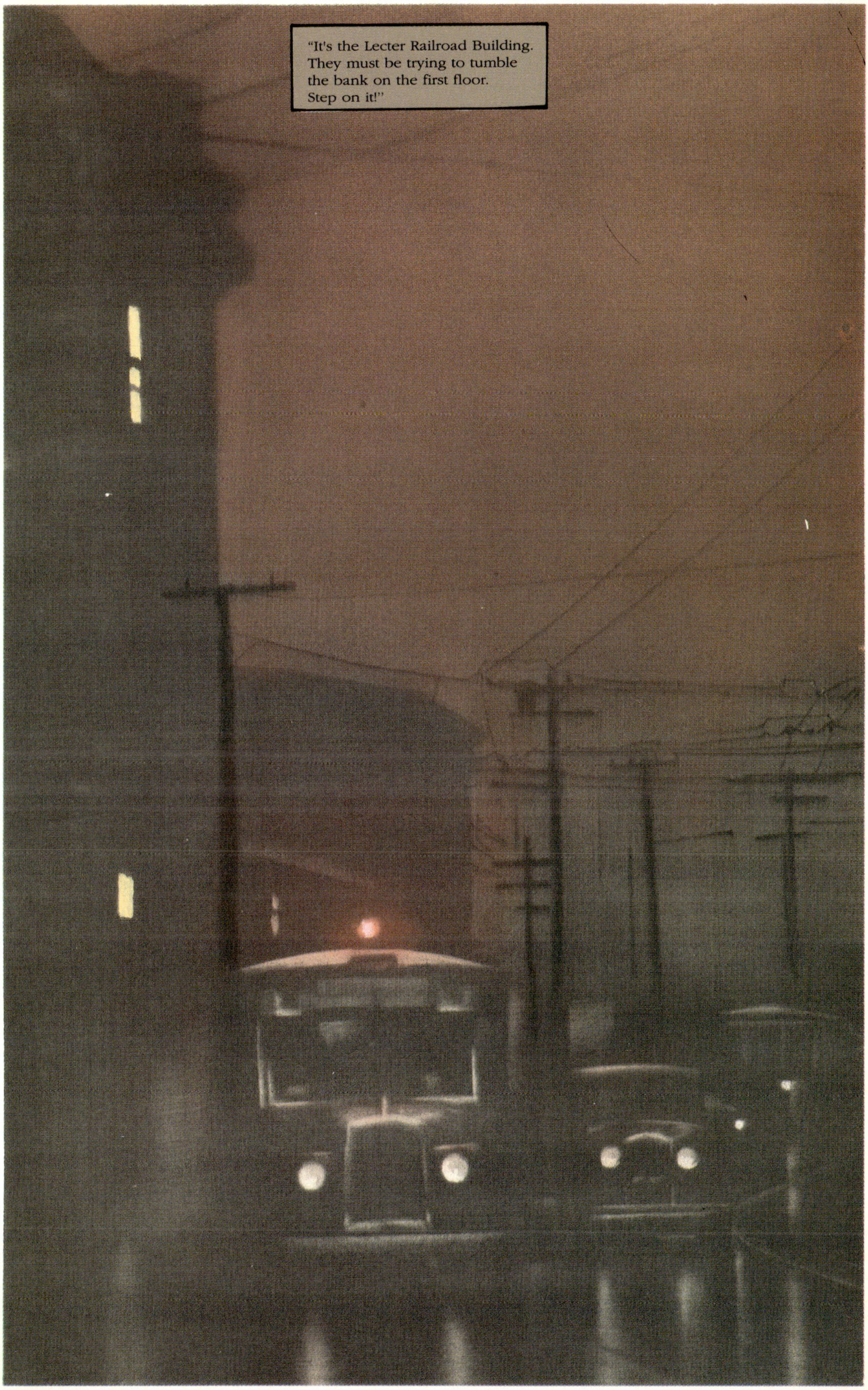
"It's the Lecter Railroad Building. They must be trying to tumble the bank on the first floor. Step on it!"

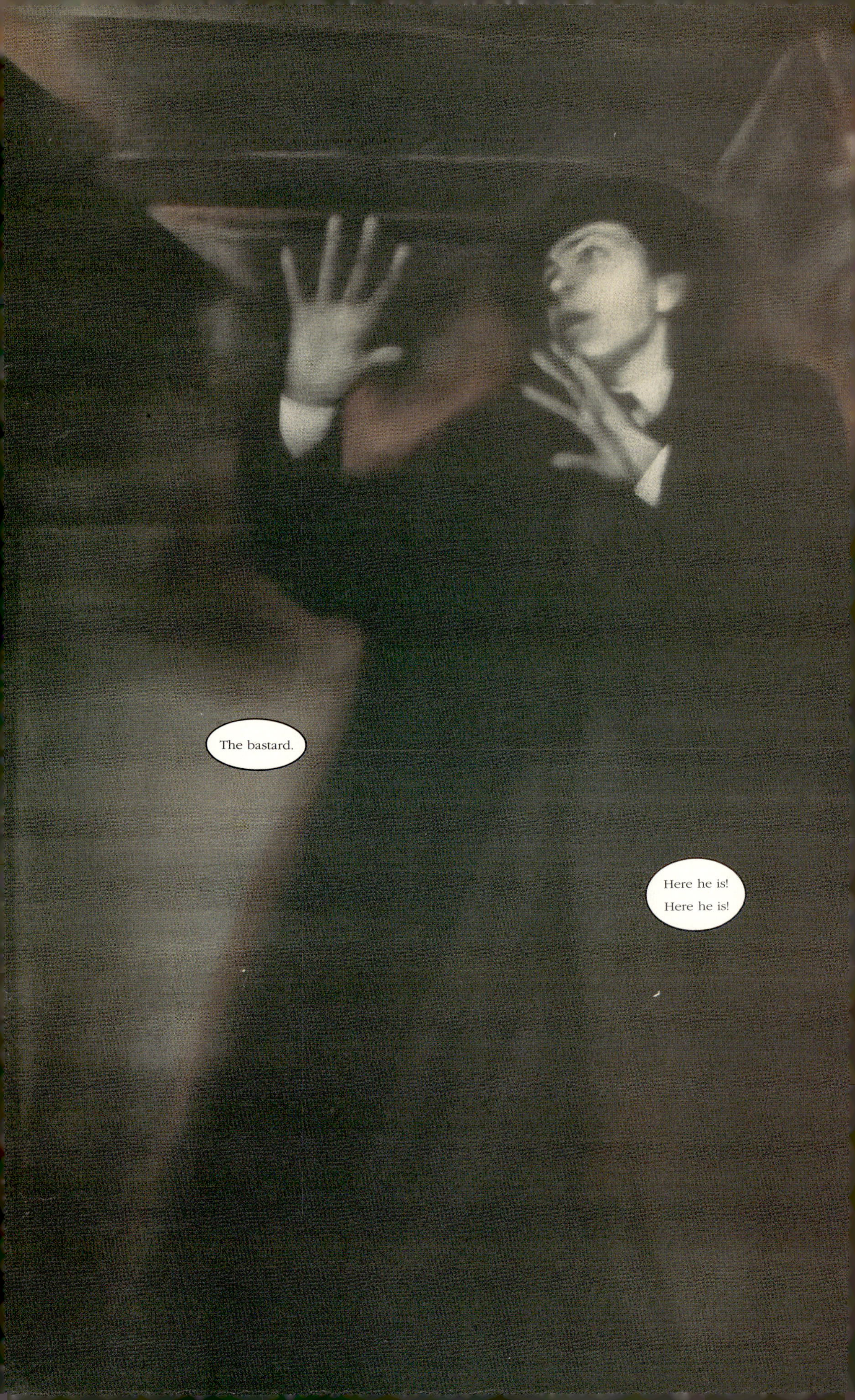
The bastard.
Here he is! Here he is!

"One never approaches Lang's films for comfort or reassurance." writes Ted Sennett in his book *Great Movie Directors*. Indeed, when one considers the body of work that makes up the career of Fritz Lang, comfort and reassurance are certainly not the adjectives which come to mind. The director who gave us the crazed master criminal in *Dr. Mabuse*, a child murderer in *M*, the angry mobs of *Fury*, and the eternally tormented old man in *Scarlet Street* was clearly not endeavouring to make us view our world as benevolent or our fellow man as benign. Yet this was not a director who considered either himself or his films to be negative in attitude. This was a man who directed films with intense attention to every detail. This detailed approach brought him repeated triumphs in Germany, and while it brought him much success in America as well, it also brought him a reputation in Hollywood as a tyrant of the first order.

Friedrich Christian Anton Lang was born in Vienna on December 5, 1890. His father Anton Lang was a native of Vienna and a municipal architect. His mother Paula was Jewish-a catholic convert from Moravia. The years of Lang's childhood were the greatest period of Austrian history. It was a time of great opulence and glamour for those who were wealthy enough to be a part of it. His feelings and impressions about his schooling, his parents, or the world in which he grew up can only be guessed at, as he never gave interviews on matters concerning his personal life of this, or any other, period. Lang left home at the age of eighteen and travelled to Belgium where for a time he lived rather a Bohemian existance, sketching picture postcards for money. Around 1910 he went on a sea voyage which took him to points in Africa, the Pacific, and Asia. Upon his return, to Paris, he attended a school to learn painting. It was during this period that he first began watching movies regularly. The idea of not just painting pictures, but making them move was a fascination which began during these days in Monmatre, and became his life.

In mid-July of 1914 Archduke Franz Ferdinand was assassinated and a chain of events was set in motion which led to the outbreak of what came to be known as the First World War. At the outbreak of hostilities Lang returned to Vienna where he was recruited as a Lieutenant in the Austrian army. It was while he was recuperating from his wounds in Vienna that he began writing stories and film scripts. He met Joseph May, a Viennese film producer and wrote a story for a film which May produced and directed. Also during this time, Lang was observed performing in a play by Erich Pommer, who was head of one of Germany's largest film companies. He offered Lang a position with his company Decla. Lang went to work for Pommer writing screenplays for several films. He felt that he could do better than the directors for whom he was writing, so he convinced a reluctant Pommer to allow him to try his hand at directing. Fritz Lang's directorial debut was with the film *Halblut* (Halfbreed) 1919. This, and Lang's second film, *Der Herr der Liebe* (The Master of Love) 1919, convinced Pommer that Lang possessed true artistic talent.

In *Das Wandernde Bild* (The Moving Image) 1920, Lang began a ten year collaboration with Thea von Harbou, whom he married on August 22, 1922. It was a close artistic collaboration which lasted until Lang's departure from Germany in 1932. There is a disagreement among Lang scholars as to the precise influence that Thea von Harbou had on Lang and the development of his work. But there can be little doubt that her influence was considerable. He certainly must have felt that von Harbou shared and understood his approach to filmmaking, and it certainly proved to be a productive artistic partnership.

It was at the outset of his first trip to America that Lang got the inspiration for one of his greatest works. His ship, the S.S. Deutschland, had docked in New York harbor. The evening before he and his party disembarked, he was strolling the deck, and stopped to observe the night lights of New York City. The flashing neon lights, and the luminous advertisements fascinated him. "At night the city did not give the impression of being alive," Lang said, "...it lived as illusions lived. I knew then that I had to make a film about all of these sensations." The result was *Metropolis*, 1927, one of the greatest spectacles in the history of the cinema. While the film garnered largely favourable reviews, it did not recoup enough of its initial investment even after foreign distribution to turn in a profit. Financially, it was a failure. While *Metropolis* has proven to be a durable classic, the film considered by many to be the greatest of Lang's German years, and certainly his finest collaboration with Thea von Harbou was *M*, 1931,. The subject matter was that of a child murderer and his pursuit by both the police and the criminal underground. Produced by independent Seymour Nebenzal, the subject was truly a daring one on which to base a film. Although Lang later denied that he had based his film on the deadly exploits of the Dusseldorf child murderer Peter Kurten (the script was completed before Kurten had been apprehended), the notoriety of that case no doubt added to the power of the film in its intial release. Not only was the subject itself a gamble, but so was the use of Peter Lorre for the main role of Beckert; the child murderer to whom the title refers. Lorre was a talented and sought-after actor on the German theater stage, but he had never done a motion picture before. The film was originally to be titled *Morder Unter Uns* (the Murderer Among Us), and when Lang tried to rent Staaken Zepplinhalle film studio for the production, he was denied permission. When he met the studio manager in person and at one point became irritated with the man and grabbed him by his tie, he noticed a swastika pin on the tie. Lang then understood: the manager was a member of the Nazi Party, and misunderstood that original title to be a reference to the Nazis. When Lang explained to him that the film was to be about a child murderer, the man was greatly relieved, and immediately opened his studio.

By this time the political situation in Germany had heated to the boiling point, as the fragile government of the Weimar Republic had been unable to stabilize itself. On March 11th, 1931, Hitler appointed Joseph Goebbels as Minister of Propaganda, which gave Goebbels jurisdiction over all film production in Germany. Clearly, the cultural world in Germany was on the verge of a change for the worse. The same changes had been going on for some time in the relationship between Fritz Lang and his wife Thea von Harbou. Although their artistic partnership had recently yielded its finest work yet, by 1933 the two had, according to Lang, grown apart on a personal level. Although they shared important artistic beliefs, von Harbou had grown up in Bavaria, and thus had always held strong German nationalist sentiments. Lang by contrast had been born in Vienna.

Lang received a call to meet with Goebbels at his office in the Propaganda Ministry. To Lang's astonishment, Goebbels offered to make him the leader of German film production in the Third Reich. Lang, who recalled sweating heavily throughout the appointment, dared to remind the Minister that he had Jewish ancestry on his mother's side. Goebbels assured him that in view of the director's fine record in the Great War (he was decorated for bravery), this matter of Jewish ancestry could be overlooked. Lang, of course, had no intention of even considering the offer. He told Goebbels that he would like twenty-four hours in which to consider the offer, and Goebbels agreed. Lang then went home, packed up some jewelry, and as much money as he could, and boarded a night train for Paris. Thea von Harbou stayed behind, and took a position in the film industry of the Third Reich, but she never reached the creative level that she had with Lang either with the Nazis, or after their defeat. She would die of head injuries sustained in a fall in 1954. Fritz Lang would not return to Germany for twenty-five years.

BRIAN BOLTEN
excerpts from his essay "Fritz Lang"

People who provided uncommon inspiration, help, or wisdom during the produktion of M 3:
ALLEN SPIEGEL; STACEY & CATHY WOOLLEY; MIKE JOHNSON; DAVE SOFRANKO,
KEVIN EASTMAN, PHILIP NUTMAN, MARK BODÉ, JON BRAY, BALLARD BORICH;
ANNAMARIE BORICH; BILL SMART; TARA DALY; T.A. BOYLE; BRIAN BOLTEN;
RANDY SANDLER, STEVE NILES; JAN MULLANEY; JEFFREY MUTH; STACIE HARTZ;
STUART WOOLLEY; RUTH RUBENSTEIN; ELIZABETH MUTH; RILEY HUMLER;
RICHARD KATZ; ANNA; DEMIAN HUMLER; TIM BOYLE; WALTER SIMONSON;
CINCINNATI ART GALLERIES; THE EMERY CENTER; TUNDRA PUBLISHING, INC;
GERHARD RICHTER; SIR DAVID LEAN; JOEL & ETHAN COEN; ANTHONY HOPKINS.
Cover Transparencies RILEY HUMLER / CINCINNATI ART GALLERIES
Research & 2nd Unit Photography JULIANNA MUTH; MIKE JOHNSON
Photography Assistant CATHY WOOLLEY
Consulting Editors VALARIE JONES; FRED BURKE
Editor-in-Chief CATHERINE YRONWODE
Publisher DEAN MULLANEY

Art & Script, Copyright © 1990 JON J MUTH
all the artwork reproduced in this book is done in silverpoint, graphite, pastel, and charcoal on prepared paper
all of the work was based on original photographs – *with the exception of page 41* – but no photographs are reproduced herein

Published by
ECLIPSE BOOKS, P.O. BOX 1099, FORESTVILLE, CALIFORNIA 95436

NEXT:
THE TRIAL

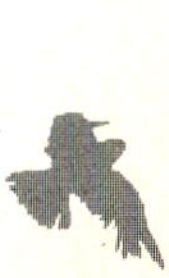